Creative Co

withou

Wheat, Milk

Creative Cooking
without
Wheat, Milk and Eggs

Ruth R. Shattuck

South Brunswick and New York: A. S. Barnes and Company
London: Thomas Yoseloff Ltd

A. S. Barnes and Co., Inc.
Cranbury, New Jersey 08512

Thomas Yoseloff Ltd
108 New Bond Street
London W1Y OQX, England

Library of Congress Cataloging in Publication Data

Shattuck, Ruth R
    Creative cooking without wheat, milk, and eggs.

    1. Cookery for allergics.   I.   Title.
RM221.A6S48   641.5'63   72-6392
ISBN 0-498-01157-7

PRINTED IN THE UNITED STATES OF AMERICA

For
Dr. Jennie I. Rowntree

Contents

Forewords

The author has prepared a systematic, orderly book on food allergies.

During the past half century excellent progress has been made in the discovery of methods for determining the primary etiologic factor in the symptoms complex—usually food sensitization. Some people eat to live; some live to eat; we are what we eat. The normal physiology, the stable emotions, the mental development, the physical body depend on a wholesome diet.

I recommend this book to all physicians, dietitians, and most definitely to people who want to prepare meals for a healthful diet.

It is a book anyone can follow with complete understanding.
Frederick L. Scheyer, M.D., F.A.C.S.

Mrs. Shattuck is a superb cook and has tested and retested these gourmet recipes. She is well qualified to write such a cookbook. She is a graduate in home economics, has served an internship in hospital dietetics, and has prepared foods for an allergic husband and a normal family for many years.

Foods delicious enough to serve the entire family will be appreciated by persons whose diets are restricted, and who do not want to be conspicuous on that account. The recipes are practical for the busy housewife, gourmet enough for appreciative guests, and appealing to children. I have had the opportunity to sample many of the recipes. I recommend this book heartily.

Jennie I. Rowntree, Ph.D.

Professor Emerita of Nutrition

Introduction

The recipes in this book are the result of over thirty years of experimentation and adaptations. Food allergies present numerous problems to the homemaker in a day when more and more people devote less and less time to the art of cooking. Wheat, milk, and eggs, alone or in combination, are found in practically all commercially produced foods. The necessity of eliminating any of them necessitates more "cooking from scratch" at home and less frequent eating in restaurants.

Wheatless or gluten-free diets are probably the most difficult and are a problem for people with the nonabsorption syndrome as well as those with allergies. Eggless or milkless living is a close second in difficulties. Eggs, milk, or wheat, or all three, seem to lurk in practically everything good to eat. The frustrations involved in attempting to prepare "normal" meals without one or more of them can be overwhelming.

These recipes are also important for those individuals with heart problems—which means that egg, milk, and fat must be restricted.

Recipes included here make it possible to serve the same menu to all, no matter what the occasion. This is important to all, but especially to children who do not want to be looked upon

11

as different. Perhaps the variations for many of the recipes will inspire you to make new taste treats of your own. It is the ability to give variety to the basic ingredients available to us that gives zest to the imposed restrictions.

Food allergies range from one to many and can change over the years. An individual with sensitive predispositions needs variety and the best possible diet within the limitations. Compensating with large amounts out of proportion to the general diet can bring on new allergic reactions. A child allergic to eggs should not be drowned in milk, but should have normal proportions of meat, bread, fruit, and vegetables, besides the milk. If an allergy to milk, wheat, or eggs develops there are other foods which should be treated with caution. Foods known to be common allergic offenders, such as chocolate, shellfish, peanuts, oatmeal, and buckwheat, are practically avoided. If properly respected and treated, food allergies in children are often outgrown. Unfortunately this is not so likely for adults. A state of general good health is important in controlling allergies, and if the general well-being is impaired by illness or fatigue the defenses are not as strong and old allergies may reappear.

When diet restrictions are necessary, boredom from the obvious simple fare can soon jade the appetite; good nutrition then becomes a problem. It is unwise to have one member of the family feel either conspicuous or neglected because of these restrictions, and special diets become tedious problems for both the "patient" and the wife or mother. Meeting the challenge of a well-nourished happy family enjoying together tasty foods that otherwise would be forbidden can be fun; the reward is the satisfaction of a job well done.

EASY CALCULATION
OF PROTEIN ADEQUACY
ON RESTRICTED DIETS

Those who have to eliminate a protein food and wonder if their needs are met should find the tables below reassuring. The first table shows the percentage of the average requirement provided by a serving of each food and the second table shows the grams of protein in each serving. If the first table is used, the total should be 100%, with the second table, 50 grams. The first table shows that a serving of meat, a pint of milk, three slices of bread, and three servings of vegetables provide enough protein without eggs. If allergy to milk is the problem, a serving of meat, a fish or meat sandwich, bread, cereal, and vegetables provide enough protein.

Recently the National Research Council drastically reduced the amount of protein formerly considered essential. While 65 grams was formerly the average standard, about 50 grams is now acceptable, with young children needing 35 to 40 grams, women 55, and men 60 to 65 grams. Pregnant and lactating women, and rapidly growing adolescents need 65 to 75 grams.

TABLE 1

PERCENT OF AVERAGE DAILY PROTEIN REQUIREMENT FURNISHED
BY SERVINGS OF DIFFERENT FOODS

Meat, 3½ oz. cooked	50
Milk, ½ pt.	16
Cheese, 1 oz. cheddar	16
Cottage cheese, 2 oz. creamed	14
Egg, 1	12
Navy beans, ½ c. cooked	16
Bread, 1 slice	5
Cereal, 1 oz.	6
Vegetables, ½ c.	1–3
Potatoes, 4 oz.	4
Fish, 3½ oz.	35

TABLE 2

GRAMS OF PROTEIN IN SERVINGS OF DIFFERENT FOODS.
AVERAGE REQUIREMENT: 50 GRAMS

Meat, 3½ oz. cooked	23–27

Milk, ½ pt.	8
Cheese, 1 oz. cheddar	8
Cottage cheese, 2 oz.	7
Bread, 1 oz. (1 slice)	2–3
Egg, 1	6
Cereal or crackers, 1 oz.	3
Navy beans, 4 oz. cooked	8
Peanut butter, 1 oz.	8
Vegetables	1–3
Gelatin dessert	2

HELPFUL HINTS AND SUGGESTIONS
FOR SUCCESS IN RECIPES

INGREDIENTS:

The quality of the finished product can be no better than the quality of the ingredients.

Flour

The purpose of sifting is to incorporate air. Some, but not all, flours on the market specify "Do not sift." When it is still necessary, an easy, quick and clean method is to stir or whip the flour in its sack or container with a fork until it is light. Then spoon gently into measuring cup. Flours vary because wheats from different parts of the country vary. These recipes, except for those specifying cake flour, are made with a hard wheat flour of a nationally advertised middlewest brand.

Baking Powder

Double action baking powder is used throughout.

Dates

Many recipes call for chopped dates or date chips.* The chips

---

* To my knowledge there is only one place to buy these. They come in 3 and 5 lb. tins and are available from Shields Date Gardens, 80–225 highway 111, Indio, California 92201. Valorie Jean Date Shop, Thermal, Calif. 92274 has date crunchies which are moist date pieces for cooking or eating. Catalogs are available.

are small pieces of top-quality dates, dried and packaged in air-tight containers. They save the time and labor of pitting and chopping, are always fresh, always top quality; are less expensive than fresh dates, and can always be on hand. To use the chips in cakes or batters, soften by steaming over boiling water. To use in sauces, soak in a little water, orange juice, or wine, depending on the combination of flavors desired.

Evaporated Milk and Non-Fat Milk

Whipped evaporated milk replaces whipped cream; it is low in cholesterol, low in calorie, and easy to keep on hand, as well as being inexpensive and completely satisfying. Directions for whipping are given with the recipes. The flavors are carefully adjusted to disguise any carmelized milk taste from the canned milk.

Whipped non-fat milk does not hold up as well as canned milk, but has a more creamlike flavor when used as a topping or re-placement for whipped cream to embellish desserts at serving time. To whip, follow directions on package; have ingredients and utensils thoroughly chilled but not whipped until just before serving time.

Grated or Chopped Orange or Lemon Peel

Generous amounts of these are used for flavoring. Frozen juice is fine for most recipes, but in order to have the peel available, *thinly* peel the rind from any orange or lemon used, whether needed immediately or not, and store in a small bottle in the freezer. A good sharp knife is your best friend for this job, or it can be cut with kitchen scissors.

Shortening

The success of many of these recipes depends on the creaming of the shortening and sugar. For best results, the creamed mixture must be *very* light and fluffy. The best way to achieve this is to start with room temperature shortening, beat by hand or in the electric mixer until it is light and fluffy. Then, and only then, slowly add the sugar, beating all the time so that the mixture never loses its fluffy texture. It should be very creamy looking. Overbeating gives the mixture a grainy appearance and the texture of the finished product will not be as light. Most of the recipes simply read "cream well together." Proper creaming is especially important where no eggs are used.

Yeast

Dry packaged yeast is used only by preference. Cake yeast can be substituted, if desired.

Carob

Carob is a chocolate substitute that comes either as a powder similar to cocoa or as a candy bar. Where allergy to chocolate occurs it is very useful. In recipes calling for cocoa, simply substitute an equal amount of carob, or 3 T. of carob can replace 3 T. of flour. To replace one square of chocolate, dissolve 3 level T. of carob powder in 2 T. water. The candy bar is sweet so it is not a replacement for bitter chocolate but can be melted or shaved. The bar contains dry skim milk, and therefore can not be used with milk allergies.

EQUIPMENT

Pastry Cloth

In many recipes a pastry cloth is suggested, and a pastry stocking on the rolling pin is also helpful. Pastries and doughs do not tend to stick as much and use less flour when these accessories are used. The doughs are also much easier to handle and are lighter in texture. The cleanup is much quicker and easier, which is important.

General Equipment

Equipment varies in every kitchen. Stoves and ovens have their eccentricities. Cookie sheets and baking pans are not all the same even in your own kitchen. Your oven may call for slight temperature changes from those specified here. Glass cooking equipment calls for a decrease of 25 degrees. All recipe temperatures are for metal. All temperatures are Fahrenheit and all measurements are for low altitude.

Clean Beaters

When only part of the mixing is done in an electric mixer, clean beaters well before continuing with a spoon. Be sure all of the material from the beaters is included in the mix, otherwise the proportions of the recipe may be changed.

ABBREVIATIONS

Teaspoon	tsp.	Baking soda	soda
Tablespoon	T.	Half and Half	½ and ½
Cup	c.	(half milk and half cream)	
Pint	pt.	Vegetable	veg.
Quart	qt.	Optional	opt.
Package	pkg.	Hour	hr.
Ounce	oz.	Minute	min.
Pound	lb.	Temperature	temp.
Gallon	gal.	Number	# or no.

Creative Cooking
without
Wheat, Milk and Eggs

English Equivalent Measures

	American	English
1 cup of breadcrumbs (fresh)	1½ oz.	3 oz.
1 cup of flour or other powdered grains	4 oz.	5 oz.
1 cup of sugar	7 oz.	8 oz.
1 cup of icing sugar	4½ oz.	5 oz.
1 cup of butter or other fats	8 oz.	8 oz.
1 cup of raisins, etc	5 oz.	6 oz.
1 cup of grated cheese	4 oz.	4 oz.
1 cup of syrup, etc	12 oz.	14 oz.

1 English pint	20 fluid ounces
1 American pint	16 fluid ounces
1 American cup	8 fluid ounces
8 American tablespoons	4 fluid ounces
1 American tablespoon	½ fluid ounce
3 American teaspoons	½ fluid ounce
1 English tablespoon	⅔ to 1 fluid ounce (approx.)
1 English tablespoon	4 teaspoons

The American measuring tablespoon holds ¼ oz. fiour

Part 1
Breads and Desserts

1
Eggless, Eggless and Milkless and Low-Fat Recipes

BREAD

Good homemade bread can be a great morale booster for re-stricted diets. It is also fun to make and need not be difficult.

ENGLISH MUFFINS AND ENGLISH MUFFIN BREAD
(eggless)
Good, easy to make, stores well frozen.

Scald   1 c. milk, Add ½ c. water, 3 T. shortening, 1½ tsp. salt
Cool to lukewarm
Dissolve   1 pkg. dry yeast in ¼ c. water. Add 1½ tsp. sugar.
Stir occasionally. When bubbly add to milk mixture in large bowl.
With heavy wooden spoon gradually beat in 4–5 c. flour. (part whole wheat if desired).

23

It should be a medium-stiff dough. Place in greased bowl. Grease top also. Cover and let rise in warm place until doubled in bulk— about one hour. Turn out onto lightly floured board or pastry cloth and with well-floured hands knead gently about 1 min. *Muffins:* Roll out dough until ¼ inch thick. Cut rounds with a large cutter such as a 2½ size tin can. Dip rounds lightly in cornmeal and place on cookie sheet. Let stand uncovered until they rise slightly -30–40 min. Preheat frying pan or griddle to 300°. Grease lightly. "Bake," uncovered and uncrowded, 15–20 min. or until underside is browned. Turn with pancake turner. Bake other side. Serve immediately, or cool on wire rack and reheat as needed. Best when split, buttered and browned under broiler. Yield: 12 muffins.
Bread: Divide dough in half. Shape gently into loaves. Sprinkle with cornmeal. Place in greased bread tins. Let rise 30–40 min. Bake at 425° 30–40 min. Cool on wire racks. Wonderful for toast. Recipe may be doubled or tripled. Double for 3 loaves of bread or 2 loaves and 8 muffins, or 24 muffins.

BATTER BREAD (eggless)
Quick, easy and good. Yield: 1 large loaf.

Scald   1 c. milk. Add 3 T. sugar, 1 tsp. salt 1½ T. shortening
Dissolve 2 pkg. dry yeast in 1 c. warm water. Stir into milk
         mixture
Add   4–4½ c. sifted flour.
Stir until well blended, about 2 min. Cover. Let rise in warm place until more than doubled in bulk—about 40 min. Pour into greased 1½ qt. casserole or pan. Bake at 375° about 1 hour.

ANNETTE'S BREAD
(eggless and milkless)

The secret of most good homemade bread is a tender dough and lots of kneading. The tendency is to add too much flour.
For 2 loaves of bread scald *2½ c. liquid*—milk, water, or potato water, or a mixture. At least half milk, when allowed, gives a

better-textured and more nutritious bread. Pour liquid into a large pan or bowl. While it cools to lukewarm, dissolve *1½ pkg. dry yeast* in *¼ c. warm water.* Stir until mixed. Let stand until bubbly and about doubled in amount. Add *3 T. sugar, 1 T. salt* and bubbly yeast to lukewarm liquid. Add *2 T. shortening.* What doesn't melt will blend in as you continue. A total of about *6 c. unsifted all-purpose flour* (part whole wheat or other grain if desired) will be needed. Add about 2 c. and stir with a big spoon until well mixed. Add 2 more c. and stir again. Now add gingerly ½–1 c. mixing until you have a very soft spongy dough. Use just enough flour so you can handle the dough on the board. Use remainder as you knead.

Turn dough onto well-floured board and with floured hands knead vigorously about 10 min., turning dough a quarter turn each time and using a one-two motion or double knead as you work. The dough will still be very soft and won't hold its shape but will be tender and springy.

Wash, dry, and grease the large container and return dough to it. Grease top lightly, cover, and let it double in bulk in a draftless warm place. When it has doubled in bulk, return to board, and using most of remaining flour knead until it squeaks and pops and is smooth and satiny. It will still be very tender. Return to pan, cover, and let double in bulk again. Return to board with just enough flour to prevent sticking.

Cut into 2 equal-sized pieces, cover, let stand for 10 min. It will spread on the board. One at a time, flatten each piece into a rectangle 10–12 inches square. Using your knuckles, pound it well. Fold over once. Pick up ends and flap it against the board several times, so as to remove the air bubbles. Now fold it over gently into thirds, folding in seam with knuckles. Turn it over, tuck in the ends, and shape until smooth.

Place in greased bread tins, cover with tea towel, let rise until doubled in bulk again. Bake in preheated oven at 425° 15 min.; reduce temperature to 375° and continue baking 30 min. or until brown and done. Remove from pans to cake racks. Butter tops of loaves (optional) and let cool.

Variations: Besides varying the grains, honey can be used instead of sugar; chopped dates, nuts, or raisins may be added; and sugar and cinnamon can be spread on dough before it is rolled.

SOURDOUGH BREADS
(eggless and milkless)

Sourdough breads can be made from either commercial or wild yeast starters. When weather conditions permit, wild yeast starters are fun to have and seem to have a better flavor. The starter must be out of doors part of each day to capture the wild yeast. A constant temperature of approximately 80° is necessary. For cooler nights put it near a pilot light, hot water heater, or furnace. Four or five days are necessary for it to ripen. Milk gives a better-flavored product than water and is faster acting, but water must be used for milk allergies.

WILD YEAST STARTER

Measure 2 c. milk or water into a wide-mouth plastic, glass, or pottery container and let stand at room temperature 24 hrs. (Omit standing for water.) Stir in 2 c. unsifted flour. Cover with nylon net or cheesecloth and expose to wild yeast. Keep warm until it is bubbly and sour—4–5 days. If it begins to crust over or dry out, add enough water to return to original consistency. Store in refrigerator, tightly covered.

As you use the starter, replace it by adding equal amounts of milk or water and flour, let stand at room temperature several hours or overnight before returning it to refrigerator. It should be used often or frozen. Allow to sit 24 hrs. at room temperature after thawing before using.

The sourness of your starter, which varies, will affect the flavor of your products and the required amounts of baking soda which acts as a second leavening. The sourer the starter the more soda is needed. Use ½–¾ tsp. but not more.

COMMERCIAL YEAST STARTER

Using same type of container as above, mix thoroughly 2 c.

warm water or milk, 2 c. flour and 1 pkg. dry yeast. Let stand 10–12 hrs. or overnight. It is now ready to use. Replenish and store as above.

FRENCH BREAD (eggless and milkless)

In a large mixing bowl combine 1½ c. warm water, 1 c. starter, 4 c. unsifted flour, 2 scant tsp. salt, 1½ tsp. sugar. Mix well. Let sit at room temperature until doubled in bulk—overnight or longer. Mix together and stir in 1 c. unsifted flour and ½ tsp. soda. Turn dough onto floured board or pastry cloth, adding up to 1 c. more flour if needed to make stiff dough. Knead until satiny 5–8 min.

Shape into 2 long loaves. Place well apart on lightly greased cookie sheet. Cover. Let rise in warm place until nearly doubled in bulk—up to 3–4 hrs. Just before baking brush with water and make diagonal slashes with a sharp knife in tops of loaves. Bake at 400° about 45 min. or until medium brown. During baking, place pan of water in bottom of oven, but don't let it cook dry. Remove bread to cake racks to cool.

SOURDOUGH ENGLISH MUFFINS AND BREAD (eggless)

In large bowl combine ½ c. starter, 1 c. milk, 2 c. unsifted flour. Mix well. Cover and let stand at room temperature overnight or about 8 hrs. It should be at least double in bulk and bubbly.

Combine and add   ½ c. unsifted flour, 1 T. sugar, ¾ tsp. salt, ½ tsp. soda.

Turn dough onto floured board or pastry cloth and proceed with kneading, cutting, etc. as for plain English muffins and bread. (See page 23) Yield: 12 muffins or 1 loaf of bread.

The muffins can be refrigerated overnight and baked the following morning if they have reached the cookie-sheet stage and are allowed to rise 30 min. before refrigeration. Keep covered. Allow 2–3 min. extra baking time on each side.

SOURDOUGH BISCUITS (eggless)

Start these in the morning to use for dinner. They are also good rewarmed. The texture is more like a roll than biscuit.

Mix together   ½ c. starter, 1 c. milk, 1 c. flour
Cover, let double in bulk in warm place.

About 1¼ hrs. before serving time mix together and add to starter
mixture   ½ c. unsifted flour, ½ tsp. salt, 1 T. sugar, 1 tsp. baking powder, ½ tsp. soda.

Turn dough out onto pastry cloth or board with 1 c. flour on it. Knead lightly, working in enough flour to give biscuit dough consistency. Roll out and cut biscuits.

Dip in mixture of melted butter and salad oil. Put in pan close together and let rise about ½ hr. Bake at 375° 30–40 min. Yield: 1–1½ doz.

SOURDOUGH PAN CORNBREAD (eggless)

Mix in bowl   ½ c. starter, ½ c. yellow cornmeal, ¼ c. un-
sifted flour, 1 T. sugar, 1 c. milk.
Let sit in warm place about one hr.
Mix together and stir in ½ c. unsifted flour, ½ c. cornmeal
½ tsp. salt, ½–¾ tsp. soda
Add   2 T. melted margarine
Pour into greased 8 × 8-inch pan. Bake at 450° 25–30 min.

SWEDISH LIMPE (eggless and milkless)

Different and appealing.
Boil together for 3 min. 2 c. water, ½ c. sugar, 1 T. shortening,
2 tsp. chopped orange peel, 1 scant tsp.
anise seed. Let cool to lukewarm.

Add and stir until dissolved 1 pkg. yeast.

Gradually add about 3 c. white flour to make a soft dough. Let rise until doubled in bulk, about 1½ hrs.

Stir down and add 1 tsp. salt and about 2 c. rye flour, or enough to make a stiff dough.

Let rise again about 2 hrs., or until doubled in bulk. Knead slightly. Shape into 1 large or 2 small loaves.

Put into greased pan, greasing top of loaf also. Let rise 30–40 min.

Bake at 350° 45–60 min., or until browned and done.

ORANGE BREAD (eggless and milkless)

Lovely for breakfast toast or sandwiches. For stronger orange flavor substitute more orange juice for portion of water.

Dissolve   1 pkg. dry yeast in 1½ c. warm water.

Add   1 c. orange juice, 3 c. unsifted flour.

Cream together ⅓ c. shortening, ½ c. sugar. Add to yeast mixture. Beat until smooth. Cover and let rise in warm place 1–1½ hrs. or until doubled in bulk.

Add   1 tsp. salt, 4 T. grated orange rind, about 4 c. unsifted flour or enough to make a soft but kneadable dough.

Knead lightly, place in well-greased bowl, cover, and let rise in warm place until double in bulk—about 1½ hrs.

Shape into loaves—2 large, 3 medium, or 1 large and 4–5 small (2½×4½). Place in well-greased tins, let rise again until light— about 1 hr.

Bake at 400° about 30 min. for small loaves, 35–40 min. for larger loaves, or until well browned and done. Grease tops and remove from pans to cool on cake rack.

The little loaves make wonderful casual gifts.

ORANGE BREAD SWEET ROLLS

Use dough for one large loaf to make about 12 sweet rolls. Roll out and proceed as for homemade mix sweet rolls. Bake at 350° 12–20 min. or until lightly browned. Cool. Frost with confectioner's icing made with orange juice.

JULE KAGA (CHRISTMAS BREAD)
(eggless)

Most Christmas bread and pastries are rich with eggs but this is rich without eggs.

Scald	1 c. milk
Stir in	½ c. sugar, 1 tsp. salt, ½ c. shortening.

Cool to lukewarm

Dissolve   2 pkg. yeast in ¼ c. warm water

Stir into lukewarm mixture

Add   2 c. sifted flour. Beat vigorously.

Cover and let rise in warm place until doubled in bulk, about 30 min. Stir down

Add, and stir in   1½ tsp. ground cardamom, ½ c. raisins. ¼ c. each chopped candied citron and cherries, ¼ c. chopped almonds (optional)

Add about   2½ c. flour.

The dough should be just stiff enough to handle. Turn out on lightly floured board or pastry cloth and knead until smooth and elastic, 10–15 min. Place in greased bowl, brush top with shortening. Cover. Let rise until doubled in bulk—about 1 hr. Punch down. Knead lightly 1–2 min.

Form into a round loaf. Place on large greased baking sheet. Cover. Let rise about 1 hr. or until doubled in bulk.

Bake at 400° for 10 min. Reduce temperature to 350°. Continue baking about 40 min. Cool on rack. Frost with confectioner's icing and decorate with more fruits and nuts.

YEAST ROLLS
Monkey Bread (eggless)

Scald   1 c. milk. Cool to lukewarm
Dissolve   1½ pkg. dry yeast in the milk

Add   4 T. sugar, 1 scant tsp. salt, ½ c. margarine, about
             3 c. flour.

Beat vigorously until well mixed. Cover and put in warm place
to rise, about 1 hr. or until doubled in bulk. Punch down and roll
out on lightly floured board until ¼ inch thick.

Cut with biscuit cutter or knife into desired shaped pieces.
Dip each piece in melted margarine or butter. Arrange pieces
overlapping in a 9-inch ring mold until half-full. Let rise until
doubled in bulk. Bake at 400° 30 min. or until golden brown.
Yield: 10–12 servings.

CRESCENT ROLLS (eggless)

Tender and moist. Good eating.

Dissolve   2 pkg. yeast in ½ c. warm water

Cream together   6 T. shortening, 2 T. sugar, 1 tsp. salt

Add   1 c. warm milk and bubbly yeast to shortening
                  mixture.

Most of the shortening won't dissolve. Don't worry.
With spoon beat in 3 c. sifted flour.

The dough should be too soft to handle. Mound it in the bowl,
cover with damp tea towel. Let rise until double in bulk, about 1 hr.

Pour onto floured board or pastry cloth and roll out into large
circle about ¼-inch thick. Cut as a pie into pieces 1½ inches at
outer rim. Roll up beginning at large end. Place on greased cookie
sheet. Cover with towel, let rise until double or almost double
in bulk.

Bake 12–15 min. at 425°. Yield 1½–2 doz. rolls.

EASY ROLLS (eggless)

Delicious fresh from the oven; excellent reheated; they freeze
well. Shape rolls as you wish. This amount should serve 15–20
persons.

Dissolve   1 pkg. yeast in ½ c. warm water

Add   1 T. sugar

Scald   1 pt. milk. Pour into large bowl
Add and mix well   3 T. shortening, 3 T. sugar, 1 tsp. salt
Cool to lukewarm; stir in yeast.
Add   4 c. sifted flour. Beat until bubbly.
Fold in   1½–2 c. more flour
Let rise about 3 times original size. It should be a very soft dough.

Pour onto floured board and roll out. Cut into desired shapes, place in greased pan or muffin tins, let rise about 1 hr.
Bake at 450° 10–15–20 min. (until golden brown) depending on size and shape of rolls.

RAPID MIX ROLLS (eggless)

Sift together   2½ c. flour, 1 tsp. sugar, 1 scant tsp. salt, ¼ tsp.
                soda.

Put ⅓ of this mixture in mixing bowl. Add 1 pkg. dry yeast. Heat to lukewarm 1 c. buttermilk. Add 3 T. soft shortening. Add buttermilk and shortening to ⅓ flour mixture and beat 2 min. at medium speed of electric mixer, scraping bowl occasionally. Stir in remainder of flour.

The dough should be just easy to handle and may take another ¼–⅓ c. flour. Knead lightly, roll out and shape as desired. Let rise until double in bulk, about 1 hr. Bake 15–20 min. at 425°, or until golden brown. Yield 1–1½ doz.

If you prefer the conventional mixing method proceed as follows: Mix soda and salt into lukewarm buttermilk. Stir in yeast. Add the soft shortening and flour. Proceed as above.

SALLY LUNN (eggless)

Light and tender but no kneading. Allow 3 hrs.
Combine   ⅓ c. sugar, 1 heaping T. shortening, 1 scant tsp. salt.
Scald   1 scant c. milk. Pour over above mixture
When lukewarm add 1 pkg. yeast dissolved in ¼ c. warm water
Add   2–3 c. flour to make soft dough.

Beat well as you add the flour. The dough will be too soft to handle. Let rise until doubled. Beat it down with a spoon. Repeat. Spoon into well-greased muffin tins until ⅔ full. Let rise again. Bake at 450° about 15 min.

POTATO REFRIGERATOR ROLLS
(eggless and milkless)

This dough will keep several days in the refrigerator. Cover well.

Dissolve   1 pkg yeast in 2 c. warm water

Add   1 c. plain mashed potatoes, 1 c. melted shortening, (part butter for flavoring if allowed), ¾ c. sugar, 1½ tsp. salt.

Cover. Let stand in warm place until bubbly, about 2 hrs.

Add about   7 c. flour to make a soft dough.

Beat well. Cover. Chill. About 1½ hrs. before serving time remove from refrigerator and shape into balls. Place in greased muffin tins. Snip tops with scissors to make a cross. Brush with melted, butter, margarine, or salad oil for milkless. Let rise until doubled in bulk. Bake at 425° 15–20 min. Yield: 3 doz. rolls.

SWEET ROLLS

Good eggless yeast sweet rolls are even more difficult to find than dinner rolls. Here are several, and different fillings and toppings can give variety.

YEAST DOUGHS
SWEET ROLLS WITH HOMEMADE MIX (eggless)

This mix can be stored, tightly covered, unrefrigerated, as a biscuit mix. It is a time and money saver. The rolls are good too! Combine as for a biscuit mix 12 c. sifted flour, 2 scant T. salt, 6 T. baking powder, 2 c. shortening. Yield: 15 c.

The rolls:

Dissolve   2 pkg. yeast in ⅓ c. warm water in large mixing bowl
Add   ⅔ c. milk, scalded and cooled to lukewarm, ½ c.
            sugar, 1 tsp. vanilla and 2 c. mix. Beat until well
            blended.

Add another 2 c. mix and turn out onto floured board or
cloth and knead lightly 10–15 times. Place in greased bowl.
Grease top also. Cover. Let rise until double in bulk about 40
min. Roll dough on pastry cloth or board into a rectangle. Spread
lightly with melted margarine and filling of your choice (see below). Roll as for jelly roll. Cut into slices ¼–½ inch thick. Place
well apart on greased cookie sheet. Let rise 40 min. Bake at
350° about 20 min. or until done. Yield: 12–16 rolls. See fruit
fillings also. Spread with confectioners icing.

FILLINGS

Cinnamon sugar mix: ⅔ c. sugar—brown or white, 2 tsp. cin-
            namon, ⅓ c. chopped nuts, raisins or dates (optional).
Danish pastry filling: ¼ c. (scant) sugar, 1 T. cornstarch, dash
            of salt. Add slowly 1 c. milk and cook until thick.
            Add vanilla or almond extract to taste.
    Streusel topping: Mix together 4 T. sugar, brown or white,
2 T. flour, ½ tsp. cinnamon. Add 2 T. margarine or butter cutting in to make a crumbly mixture.
    Confectioner's icing: Add 2 T. milk or half-and-half, ¼ tsp.
lemon, orange, or almond extract, or ½ tsp. vanilla to 1 c. sifted,
packed powdered sugar. Or substitute lemon or orange juice
for milk or cream.

BUTTER HORNS (eggless)

*These rolls are delicious—comparable to the best egg batters.
They are slightly better if butter or part butter is used.*
Scald   ½ c. milk. Add ½ c. butter or margarine, ¼ tsp. salt,
            1 tsp. sugar

Dissolve 1 pkg. dry yeast in ¼ c. warm water in medium-sized bowl.

Add lukewarm milk mixture and 2½–3 c. flour.

Use just enough flour so that you can handle the dough. When it will come away from sides of bowl, turn onto lightly floured board or pastry cloth and knead about 5 min. or until dough is satiny. Place in greased bowl. Grease top also. Cover. Let double in bulk. Punch down. Roll out on board to ½ inch thickness. Spread with another ¼ c. soft butter or margarine.

Fold dough over 4 times. Wrap tightly, chill well in refrigerator. Repeat rolling and folding 3 times more. If dough gets too soft to work before finishing the 3 rolls chill until it can be handled and continue. Let rise 30 min. Chill, roll and fold twice more.

Divide dough in half for easier handling. Roll out, spread with butter or filling, roll as for jelly roll, slice, add more filling to top if desired. Place well apart on baking sheet. Let double in bulk. Bake at 375° about 20 min. They burn easily. Yield: about 1–1½ doz.

CINNAMON ROLLS (eggless)

Unusually good: not as rich as butter horns and Dutch pastries.

In pan combine   1½ c. water, 3 T. vegetable shortening, 1 tsp. salt, ½ c. sugar. Bring to boil. Remove from heat.

Add   ½ c. evaporated milk. Cool to lukewarm.

Dissolve   2 pkg. yeast in ¼ c. warm water. Add to cooled mixture. Add 5 c. flour (approximately).

Place in bowl, cover, refrigerate about 2 hrs. or until tripled in bulk. Turn onto floured pastry cloth or board. Roll thin, about ¼ inch. Spread with melted margarine—about 2 T. Sprinkle with mixture of ¾ c. sifted sugar, white or brown, and 1 tsp. cinnamon. Chopped raisins, dates, nuts, etc. optional.

Starting with long side, roll up as for jelly roll, With sharp knife slice into ½-inch slices. Place well apart on greased cookie sheet. Cover with tea towel. Let rise about 1 hr. Bake at 425° for 12–15 min. Cool on wire rack. They are very tender and are difficult to handle while hot. Confectioner's icing optional.

HOT CROSS BUNS (eggless)

Commercial hot cross buns usually have an egg wash.

Scald   ½ c. milk. Pour into large bowl.

Mix in   ¼ c. sugar, 2 tsp. salt, ¼ c. margarine, 3 T. molasses.

Cool to lukewarm

Dissolve   2 pkg. yeast in 1⅓ c. warm water. Add to above.

Add and mix well ½ c. raisins or currants, ¼ c. chopped citron, 1 c. unsifted whole wheat flour.

Add   3–3½ c. unsifted flour to make a soft dough.

Turn out on lightly floured board or cloth; knead until dough is smooth and elastic—about 10 min. Place in greased bowl; grease top lightly also. Cover. Let rise in warm place until doubled in bulk, about 1 hr.

Punch down; turn onto lightly floured board; shape into long circular roll; cut or pinch off 18 pieces. Roll into balls, place close together in 2 greased 8 × 8-inch pans. Cover; let rise in warm place until doubled in bulk, about 45 min. Bake at 400° 20–25 min., or until medium brown. Cool on wire rack. Frost with crosses of confectioner's icing. Variation: All white flour may be used and ½ tsp. Vanilla added.

DUTCH SWEET PASTRIES (eggless)

This is not a yeast dough. The method of preparation is similar to puff paste or butter horns. They are rich and very good.

Combine   2¼ c. sifted flour, 1 T. sugar, ¾ tsp. salt

Cut in   ½ c. butter (not margarine) as for pastry

Add   ⅓ c. ice water. Mix until dough becomes a soft ball.

Roll out on lightly floured pastry cloth to ⅛ inch thickness.

Divide ½ c. cold, firm butter into thirds. Cut ½ into thin slices and arrange over ⅔ of dough. Fold the unbuttered ⅓ over the center section; then fold remaining ⅓ over first section. Seal edges. Chill until firm.

Reroll to ⅛ inch thickness; repeat process with second piece of butter—folding and chilling. Repeat again using last portion of butter. Chill again.

Use only half the dough at a time to help keep it cold. Refrigerate second half. Roll to ⅛ inch thickness again. Cut into strips 3 inches wide by 8 inches long. Using either almond paste* or Danish pastry filling which is chilled enough to hold its shape put a strip down the middle of the pastry. Fold pastry around filling brushing edges with milk to seal the roll together. Make figure 8's or letter S's or any shape desired. Brush top lightly with cream and sprinkle with sugar. Place on cookie sheet. Either bake immediately or return to refrigerator while repeating process with second half. Bake at 425° 25 min. or until lightly browned. Cool on cookie sheet.

*Add 1 T. flour to ½ c. almond paste. Blend in thoroughly.

QUICK BREADS (non-yeast)

Quick breads can be good substitutes for more time-consuming yeast breads and cookies.

STEAMED BROWN BREAD (eggless)

Mix well   1¼ c. flour, 1 tsp. salt, 2 tsp. soda
                  2 c. yellow cornmeal, 1 c. minute oats.

If raisins are desired reserve ¼ c. to mix with 1 c. seedless raisins To remainder add   1 c. molasses. 2 c. buttermilk. Add raisins. Fill 4 well-greased molds ⅔ full. 1 lb. coffee tins or No. 2½ size tins are fine. Cover tightly with foil and tie.
Steam 2 hrs. in kettle with water to ⅓ height of molds. Remove foil to cool. Serve immediately, rewarm in tin, or spread slices

with butter and put under broiler a few minutes. It freezes well also.

BAKED BROWN BREAD (eggless)

Combine   ⅔ c. brown sugar, 1 c. white flour, 2¼ c. graham flour, 1 tsp. soda

Dissolve   2 tsp. soda in ⅓ c. molasses

Add together with 2 c. buttermilk to flour. Mix all thoroughly. Raisins optional. Fill well-greased molds ⅔ full and bake at 350° 30–40 min. This can also be rewarmed or frozen.

PRUNE BREAD (eggless)

A sweet loaf, nourishing and good.

Sift together   ½ c. sugar, 2 c. sifted flour, 2½ tsp. baking powder ½ tsp. soda, ¾ tsp. salt

Add   1 c. uncooked quick oats. Mix well.

Add   2 T. melted shortening, slightly cooled, to 1¼ c. room temperature buttermilk. Add to flour

Add   1 c. diced, drained cooked prunes, ½ c. nuts (optional).

Stir just until flour mixture is moistened. Pour into well-greased floured bread pan 9 × 5 × 3 inches. Bake at 350° about 60 min. Turn out onto wire cookie rack to cool thoroughly.

DATE BREAD #1 (eggless)

Substitute chopped dates or steamed date chips for prunes in recipe above.

DATE BREAD (eggless and milkless)

This bread can be used as cake also.

To   1 c. chopped dates or steamed date chips

Add   ¾ c. boiling water, ½ c. firmly packed brown sugar
                ¼ c. margarine or vegetable shortening. Stir. Let
                cool.
Add   1 tsp. vanilla
Sift together   1¾ c. sifted flour, ¾ tsp. salt, 1 tsp. soda
                2½ tsp. baking powder. Add to above mixture.
                Stir until mixed.
Put into well-greased and floured 8 × 4 × 3 inch or 9 × 5 × 3 inch
pan. Bake at 350° 1¼ hrs. Turn out on wire rack. Cool thor-
oughly. The smaller pan is better if available.

BANANA BREAD (eggless and milkless)

Cream together ⅓ c. vegetable shortening, ⅔ c. sugar
Sift together   1¾ c. sifted flour, ⅓ tsp. salt
                2 tsp. baking powder, ¼ tsp. soda
Add alternately with 1 c. mashed ripe banana (2 large or 3 small)
   Mix until smooth. Pour into 8 × 4 × 3- inch pan greased and
lightly floured. Bake at 350° 50–60 min. Cool on wire rack 10–
15 min. before removing from pan. Complete cooling and store
overnight before cutting.

CRACKED WHEAT BREAD (eggless)

   Very similar to a well-known bread served in a Seattle hotel
for many years. Lovely served with cream cheese and marmalade.
Put in bowl   ½ c. quick cooking cracked wheat or Ala (bulgar)
Add   2½ c. buttermilk
Cover and chill at least 6 hrs.
Blend in   ½ c. light molasses.
Mix well   3 c. unsifted wholewheat flour, 1 tsp. salt,
               2 tsp. soda, ½ c. white flour.
   Add to buttermilk mixture, stirring just enough to moisten
mixture evenly. Pour into greased 9 × 5 × 3-inch pan. Bake at

300° 1½ hrs. or until bread tests done with a toothpick. Let cool 5 min. then turn onto wire rack and let cool about 1 hr. before cutting. Cut thin slices. For small loaves bake in 2½ × 4½-inch tins, 45–50 min.

CRUSTY CORN CAKES (eggless and gluten free)

A welcome change from pancakes, good as a main breakfast course or as a luncheon dish topped with creamed meat or fish. Quick and easy.

Put   2–3 T. flour, or 2 T. cornstarch or potato starch flour in bottom of 1 c. measuring c. Fill with yellow cornmeal

Sift together with 2 T. sugar, ½ tsp. salt, ¼ tsp. soda, 1 tsp. baking powder. Add all at once 1 scant c. buttermilk.

Cook as pancakes immediately after adding buttermilk.

BAKED CORNBREAD (eggless and gluten free)

Double recipe above using 1⅔–1¾ c. buttermilk. Pour into well-greased muffin tins or 8 × 8-inch pan. Bake at 425° about 15 min. or until done. The square pan will take 20–25 min.

SWEDISH FLATBREAD (eggless and gluten free*)

Crispy thin rounds of bread, especially good with salads or soups, in smaller sizes good with hors d'oeuvres; a cracker substitute for gluten free.

Mix together   3 c. unsifted flour*, 3½ T. sugar, ½ tsp. salt, ½ tsp. soda

Cut in   ¼ lb. margarine until it resembles fine crumbs

Add   1 c. buttermilk.

Stir until mixture holds together like biscuit dough. Shape into a ball with hands. Pinch off pieces the size of a walnut. On floured pastry cloth roll into very thin circles. Space slightly apart

---

* For gluten-free flour substitution see page 111.

on ungreased cookie sheet. Bake at 400° 5–8 min. They should be golden brown when done.

They will not be crisp if underbaked. Store in airtight container. They freeze well. Yield about 3 doz.

BISCUITS

Biscuit mixes, both regular and extra rich, allow great versatility for restricted diets plus being easy, quick, and economical.

HOME-MADE BISCUIT MIXES

In large bowl mix together for Regular Mix   Extra-rich Mix

Regular Mix	Extra-rich Mix
8 c. sifted flour	6 c. unsifted flour
4 T. baking powder	3 T. baking powder
1⅓ T. salt	1 T. salt

Cut in until mixture resembles coarse meal

1¼ c. shortening	1¼ c. shortening

For each 2 c. of mix add

⅔–¾ c. milk	½ c. milk

This should make a soft dough but easy to handle. Turn onto floured board, knead several times, roll and use as desired. Bake biscuits at 450° 12–15 min.

To make:

Upside Down Orange Biscuits: Place cut biscuits on mixture of: ⅓ c. firmly packed brown sugar, 1 T. undiluted frozen orange juice concentrate, 1½ T. melted margarine.

Bake at 400° 15–18 min. or until done. Invert onto serving plate while still hot. Or: Boil together for 1 min. ¼ c. margarine, ¼ c. orange juice, ½ c. sugar, 2 tsp. grated orange rind.

Proceed as above.

Butterscotch Rolls: Heat together just to melt, 3 T. margarine, 3 T. water, ½ c. firmly packed brown sugar, 1 T. light corn syrup. Spoon into muffin tins or pan. Add ½ c. each chopped nuts, raisins, or date chips (optional). Roll dough as for jelly roll, seal edges, cut into 1-inch slices, place on sugar mixture. Bake at 375° 15–20 min. Invert onto serving plate while hot.

Tutti Frutti Biscuits or Rolls: Add ½ c. candied fruit and raisins, ¼–½ c. chopped nuts, and 1 T. sugar to rich mix.

Proceed as with regular biscuits. Frost warm biscuits with confectioner's icing. Top with additional fruit. Or, roll out as for biscuits, cut into 1-inch wide and 6–8-inch long strips. Roll in sugar. Twist into figure eights. Bake at 450° about 12 min. Yield: about 1 doz.

Apple Streusel Coffee Cake: Make rich biscuit dough. Pat into 8-inch cake pan. Sprinkle with ½ c. streusel mix (see page 34). Press apple slices into mixture so that they are slightly overlapping. Sprinkle more streusel over apples. Bake at 400° 10 min. with another pan or foil covering the cake. Remove cover, continue baking at 375° another 10–15 min., or until done.

SOUR CREAM MUFFINS (eggless)

In a medium-sized mixing bowl mix together until sugar is dissolved

> ¼ c. firmly packed light brown sugar, ¼ tsp. cinnamon, ¾ c. commercial sour cream, ⅓ c. milk, 1 T. melted margarine, ½ c. date chips. (for fresh dates cut milk to ¼ c.

In small bowl sift 1⅓ c. sifted flour, 2 tsp. baking powder, ½ tsp. salt. Add to sugar mixture. Stir until moistened. Spoon into well-greased muffin tins. Bake at 400° 20–25 min. Serve hot. Yield 10–12.

PLAIN MUFFINS (eggless)

Sift together   2 c. sifted flour, 1–2 T. sugar, 1 T. baking powder, 1 tsp. salt.

Pour   ⅓ c. vegetable oil, ⅔ c. milk into measuring cup.

Do not mix. Pour all at once into flour mixture. Stir quickly with fork until dough balls in the bowl. Spoon into greased muffin tins filling ⅔ full. A spoon of jam can be spooned into flattened top (optional). Bake at 475° about 10 min.

CAKES

Eggless cakes present special problems. To overcome the magic quality that eggs give to the texture and body of cakes, a quality that is taken so for granted by the average cook, requires special care and precautions.

Cakes made from scratch are the best. Creaming the shortening is very important and is best done in an electric mixer. Use the small bowl for small amounts to insure maximum creaming and transfer to a larger bowl if necessary. Cream until it is feather-light but not grainy before adding sugar. Then clean beaters well and add liquid and flour by hand.

These cakes are more fragile than those containing eggs and must be handled with great care. It is best to line the pans with greased and floured (or try powdered sugar) waxed paper, and sometimes even the shape and size of the pan makes a difference. Be sure cake is thoroughly done before removing from oven or it may fall even after it has been removed. Opening the oven door or testing for doneness prematurely will also make it fall.

There are at least two nationally advertised cake mixes which give very satisfactory results when it is not feasible to start from scratch. Omit eggs. (Don't try a mix that calls for more than two eggs.) Add 1 tsp. baking powder to the mix. Measure liquid according to directions on package. Add ½ tsp. unflavored gelatin and let stand several minutes. Add gelatin liquid all at once to cake mix and beat 3 min. in mixer. The batter will be quite stiff and seems to have greater volume. Divide between prepared cake pans. Bake on second shelf in oven. It may take a little longer than package directions. When done, remove to cake rack. Let rest about 5 min. Invert and remove waxed paper. Finish cooling.

EGGLESS POUND CAKE

This is my jewel. It is easy and adaptable. The texture is quite similar to a pound cake if it is made in an 8-inch square pan and it can be substituted for pound cake, angel food, or lady fingers as the basis of many fancy desserts. It is good plain, lovely with frosting or sauce, with fruits, drizzled with wine or liqueur, or as a base for refrigerator desserts which are given under that heading.

The basic recipe:

Cream well   ½ c. shortening. Add 1 c. sugar and then 1 tsp. vanilla or rum or ½ tsp. lemon or orange extract.

Sift together   2 c. sifted cake flour, ½ tsp. soda, 1 tsp. baking powder, ½ tsp. salt

Add alternately with 1 c. milk

Bake in 8 × 8-inch pan, greased and lined with greased and floured waxed paper, at 350° for 35–40 min., or use two 8- or 9-inch round lined pans and bake 25–30 min.

Variation: Spice Cake. Add 1½ tsp. pudding spice or your own mix, and 1 c. chopped raisins, dates, nuts, or mixture as desired.

Finger Tips: Cut square cake into small pieces, cover with icing, roll in cocoanut, chopped nuts or grated chocolate.

Cake Rum Royal: Cut cake in squares, top with ice cream, spoon over all hot rum sauce. (See sauces.) Delicious! Foamy orange sauce is yummy too.

Broiled Peach Topping: Use about 1½ c. fresh or canned peaches. Dip fresh slices in lemon juice to prevent discoloring. Arrange on baked cake set on ovenproof platter. In a quart saucepan melt ½ c. margarine or butter. Mix in ¾ c. firmly packed brown sugar, ½ c. moist cocoanut, 2 T. half and half, and 1 tsp. almond extract. Pour gently over peaches immediately. Broil several minutes or until topping is bubbly and beginning to brown. Cool.

CHOCOLATE CAKE (eggless)

Chocolate is probably the most difficult of the eggless cakes.

This one is moist with a texture very much like package mixes made with egg.

Cream   4 T. shortening. Add 1 c. sugar

Put   2 T. cornstarch in bottom of 2 c. measurer. Add enough flour to make 1¾ c.

Sift together with 3 T. cocoa, 1 tsp. baking powder, 1 scant tsp. salt. Add alternately with ¾ c. canned milk, ½ c. water, 1 tsp. vanilla. Line 8 × 8-inch pan with waxed paper, greased and floured. Put in batter, bake at 350° 35–40 min. Remove to cake rack, remove waxed paper and cool.

CHOCOLATE CAKE (eggless and milkless)

Sift together   2¼ c. cake flour, 1½ c. sugar, 1½ tsp. soda, ½ tsp. salt and 3 T. cocoa.

Mix and add   ½ c. plus 1 T. salad oil, 2 T. vinegar, 2 tsp. vanilla, 1½ c. cold water.

Pour into greased and floured 9 × 13 × 2-inch pan. Bake at 350° 30 min. Cool 15 min. and then frost with the following:

Mix in pan   1 c. sugar, 3 T. cornstarch, 3 T. cocoa, dash of salt. Add 1 c. hot water.

Cook, stirring constantly until thick. Remove from heat.

Add   3 T. butter or shortening, 2 tsp. vanilla.

PUMPKIN CAKE (eggless and milkless)

Moist and tasty, this makes an excellent holiday fruit cake. Other combinations of fruit may be used. Canned pumpkin varies in quality and flour adjustment may be necessary. This is made from a firm-textured brand.

Cream well   4 T. shortening. Add 1 c. sugar gradually.

To   2 T. cornstarch add flour to make 2 c.

Sift together with 1 tsp. *each* cinnamon, nutmeg, soda, and baking powder, ½ tsp. salt

Add alternately with 1 scant c. pumpkin mixed with enough orange juice to make 1⅓ (about ½ c. juice)

Mix until smooth. Then add 1 c. mixed candied fruit, 1½ T. chopped orange peel, 1 c. chopped nuts (optional)
Bake 1 hr. at 350° in greased loaf pan. Cool on cake rack after removing from pan.
Variation: Tomato Soup Cake. Use 2 c. plain flour; substitute 1 c. condensed tomato soup for pumpkin-orange juice; add 1½ T. chopped lemon or orange peel and 1 c. raisins for mixed fruit.

APPLESAUCE CAKE
(eggless and milkless)

Cream well   ½ c. shortening. Add gradually 1 c. sugar
Dust   1 c. raisins and ½ c. chopped nuts with 2 T. flour
              1 tsp. *each* salt, cinnamon, and nutmeg.
Mix well and add to creamed mixture.
Dissolve   1 tsp. soda in 1 tsp. warm water. Pour into 1 c. unsweetened thick tart applesauce. (Lemon juice may be added if needed.)
Beat until applesauce is foamy. Stir into shortening mixture. Add about 2 c. sifted flour. The batter should be fairly stiff. Bake in greased and floured 9 × 5 × 3-inch loaf pan at 350° about 1¼ hrs., or until it tests done with a toothpick. Candied fruit may be substituted for the raisins. Remove from pan and cool on cake rack.

GINGER COOKIE CAKE (eggless)

In a sauce pan scald 1 c. milk
Add   ½ c. margarine, ½ c. sugar, ⅓ c. molasses. Cool in large bowl
Mix together 2 c. sifted flour, ¾ tsp. soda, 1 T. cocoa, ½ tsp. salt, ¼ tsp. each ginger and nutmeg, ⅛ tsp each allspice and cloves, 1 tsp. cinnamon.
Add to above in 3–4 additions. Beat well each time.
Use a large greased shallow pan. Batter should not be deeper

than ½ inch. Bake at 375° about 15 min. Cool in pan on cookie rack. While it is still warm, spread with a lemon sugar icing made by adding ¼ tsp. lemon extract and about 2 T. milk or half and half to 2 c. sifted powdered sugar. When cool cut into squares.

CHOCOLATE SURPRISE CAKE (eggless)

This is a tender and moist cake made with pudding and cake mixes. Commercial eggless pudding mix or homemade cornstarch pudding, each using 2 c. milk, may be used.

Make a recipe of chocolate pudding according to directions. To the hot pudding add 1 pkg. chocolate or fudge cake mix, stirring until mixed. Pour into greased and floured 13 × 9 × 2-inch pan. Sprinkle top with ½ c. each semisweet chocolate chips and chopped nuts. Bake at 350° 30 35 min. Serve warm or cold, plain or with whipped or ice cream.

Variations: Combine other flavor cake mixes and puddings and vary toppings with cocoanut, streusel, butterscotch bits, and nuts.

ORANGE CAKE (eggless)

Cream until very light ½ c. shortening adding ¾ c. sugar

Add   2 tsp. grated orange rind

Sift together   3 c. sifted cake flour, 1 tsp. salt, 4 tsp. baking powder, 1¼ tsp. soda.

Add alternately with ⅔ c. orange juice mixed with ½ c. buttermilk. This makes a rather stiff batter. Pour into 2 greased and floured 8 × 8-inch pans with removable bottoms, or pans greased, lined with greased and floured waxed paper. Bake at 350° 30–35 min. or until cake pulls away from sides of pan. Cool on cake racks about 30 min. and then remove very carefully. Frost with orange butter icing and dribble with melted chocolate.

PIE CAKE TARTLETS (eggless)

These make a special occasion of a picnic or replace petit fours for the most auspicious occasions. They freeze beautifully.

Combine as for pie crust 1½ c. sifted flour, ½ c. powdered sugar,
¼ tsp. salt. Cut in 10 T. cold margarine. Add 4 T.
ice water.

When dough sticks together, form into ball and chill 1 hr. or
until firm. Then divide in half and refrigerate half. Roll as for
pie crust. Cut into circles to fit muffin tins. Do as little rolling and
handling as possible. Keep any filled muffin tins chilled while
working. Repeat with second half. Prick bottoms with fork. Bake
at 450° about 8 min. or until slightly browned. Do not overbake.
Reset oven control at 350° as you remove the tart shells.

Fill with eggless pound cake mixture and bake about 20–25
min. or until golden brown. Cool on racks. Remove carefully.
Variations: For the crust substitute part orange juice for the water
and add grated orange rind. Substitute sweetened cocoa for ½ of
powdered sugar. Flavor cake to complement the crust.
Serve plain, frosted, or topped with whipped cream.

RAISIN CAKE (eggless and milkless)

Boil together for 3 min. 1 c. packed brown sugar, 1¼ c. water
½ tsp. nutmeg, 2 tsp. cinnamon, ¼ tsp. cloves
⅓ c. shortening, 2 c. seedless raisins. Cool.

Mix   1 tsp. soda, 2 tsp. water. Add to cooled mixture.
Sift together 2 c. sifted flour, 1 tsp. salt, 1 tsp. baking powder.
Stir in. Add, if desired ½ c. chopped nuts.
Pour into greased and floured 9 × 9 or 9 × 5-inch pan. Bake at
350° about 55 min. for square pan, 1½ hrs. for bread pan. Frost
with lemon or vanilla icing.

CRANBERRY ORANGE CAKE
(eggless and milkless)

The texture of this cake is much like a steamed pudding,
tender and moist, but it takes less time than steamed pudding

and can share the oven with other things. Serve with lemon, orange, or vanilla sauce.

Sift together   3 c. sifted flour, ½ c. sugar, 1 T. baking powder, ½ tsp. *each* soda, salt, and ginger, 2 tsp. cinnamon

Add   1 T. grated orange rind, 2 c. whole cranberries

Combine   ¾ c. light molasses, ½ c. each orange juice and warm water, ¼ c. margarine, melted.

Stir into flour mixture and mix well. Add ½ c. chopped nuts. Bake in greased 13 × 9 × 2-inch pan at 350° for 40–50 min. Best served warm. Can be reheated.

SPICE CAKE (eggless and milkless)

A large moist cake which keeps well. Bake it in a tube pan, an angel food pan, or two 8-inch tube salad molds. The recipe can be cut in half.

Boil together gently for 5 min. 2 c. sugar, 2 c. water, ¾ c. shortening, 2 c. raisins, chopped dates, or steamed date chips, 1 tsp. each of cloves, allspice, nutmeg, and cinnamon.

Remove to large bowl and let cool a little.

Dissolve   1 tsp. soda in 1 T. hot water. Add to above.

Sift together and add 3½ c. flour, 2 tsp. baking powder, ¼ tsp. salt

Fold in   1 c. chopped nuts (optional)

Bake in greased tube pan at 350° for 40–50 min. or until center springs back when touched.

COOKIES

DUTCH SHORTBREAD (eggless)

Shortbread is rich and best made with butter. Where margarine gives almost as good results, a choice is indicated.

Cream until very light ¾ c. soft butter or margarine

Add gradually   ½ c. sugar, then 1 tsp. vanilla or rum or ½ tsp.
                   almond, orange, or lemon extract
Stir in   1⅔ c. unsifted flour, 2 T. milk.

Mix with hands lightly until you have a smooth dough. Wrap in waxed paper. Chill about 1 hr.

Divide dough into 4 parts. Leave quarters you are not working with in refrigerator. Cut each quarter into 8 equal slices. Roll lightly with hands into a strand about 8 inches long. Fold like a pretzel or figure 8. Brush lightly with half-and-half. Sprinkle with sugar or cinnamon and sugar. Bake at 400° about 8 min. or until lightly browned. Remove to racks to cool.

BROWN SUGAR SHORTBREAD
(eggless)

Cream well   1 c. (½ lb.) soft butter or margarine. Add 1 tsp.
                   vanilla
Add gradually   1¼ c. sifted and firmly packed brown sugar
Add   2½ c. sifted flour. Mix until smooth.

Shape into a ball, wrap tightly in waxed paper, and refrigerate until chilled, about 1 hr. Roll out on lightly floured board or pastry cloth to ¼ inch thickness. Cut into desired shapes. Bake on greased or Teflon baking sheet at 300° about 20 min. Yield, depending on size and shape of cookies, about 3 doz.

LACE COOKIES

Some lace cookies are rolled and some are drop, but the texture of the finished cookies is very much alike. They are very thin and crispy wafers and some do indeed resemble lace.

GERMAN OATMEAL LACE COOKIES
(eggless)

Combine in small pan ⅔ c. quick-cooking oats, ¼ c. flour, ¼ tsp.
       each salt, cloves and ginger, ½ c. white or brown
       sugar, 2 T. half-and-half, ½ c. margarine.

Cook over medium heat, stirring, until mixture begins to bubble, and is well mixed. Remove from heat, drop by level tsps. onto lightly greased cookie sheet. Keep well apart. They spread to 3–4 inches. Bake at 350° 3–7 min. or until lightly browned. Remove from baking sheet when firm enough to handle. Leave flat or roll into cornucopias. If you are shaping them, heavy foil makes handling easier. Cool on wire rack.

ORANGE CRACKLE COOKIES (eggless)

Excellent flavor.

Melt over low heat in 1½ qt. pan ¼ lb. butter. Cool slightly.
Thoroughly blend in 1 c. sugar.
Add thawed but undiluted 1 6 oz. can frozen orange juice. Mix well.
Sift together and add 3 c. flour, ½ tsp. soda.

Turn out on floured cloth and knead until well blended. Roll out to ⅛-inch thickness. Cut into 2-inch rounds. Place on greased cookie sheet. Glazed fruit may be used as garnish. Bake at 375° 10–12 min. or until golden brown. Remove to cooling racks immediately.

COCOANUT MOLASSES COOKIES
(eggless and milkless)

Mix together in bowl 2 c. sifted flour, ⅔ c. sugar, ¾ tsp. each baking powder and salt, ¼ tsp. soda
Cut in ⅓ c. shortening until it resembles cornmeal
Mix in grinder or blender 1 c. shredded cocoanut, ⅓ c. nuts.
Add to flour mixture. Mix well.
Stir in ⅓ c. molasses, 6 T. water.

Pinch off dough to make 1-inch balls, rolling in hands, then flatten to about ¼-inch thickness. Place on greased cookie sheet. Bake at 450° 5–7 min. or until *light* golden brown. Cool on cookie rack. Store in airtight container. Yield: 3½–4 doz.

RAISIN SQUARES (eggless)
Moist and good. Liked by all ages. They keep well.

Cream together well ½ c. shortening, 1 c. sugar. Add 3 T. light
        corn syrup
Sift together 2⅔ c. flour, ¼ tsp. mace, ¾ tsp. soda, 1 tsp. salt
Add alternately with ½ c. milk, ½ tsp. lemon extract
Blend in   1¼ c. raisins.

   Chill until easy to handle. Divide in halves. Grease and flour large cookie sheet. Roll dough directly on cookie sheet to ¼-inch thickness or less. Keep edges straight. Bake at 400° 7–10 min. or until lightly browned and done. Cut into 2-inch squares while hot and remove to cookie rack to cool. Yield: about 4 doz.
Variations: Substitute ½ tsp. cinnamon for mace, 1 tsp. vanilla for lemon, 1½ c. chopped dates for raisins.

EGGLESS SUGAR COOKIES
   A good substitute for the all-time favorite.
Cream together   ½ c. margarine, 1½ c. sugar (½ brown op-
        tional)
Add   1 tsp. vanilla
Dissolve 1 tsp. soda in ½ c. buttermilk
Add alternately to above with 3 c. sifted flour, 1 tsp. nutmeg, ½
        tsp. salt.

   Mix well. Roll out on lightly floured board or pastry cloth to about ¼-inch thickness. Cut into desired shapes with cookie cutters or place whole piece on greased cookie sheet. Top may be sprinkled with sugar or cinnamon and sugar before baking. Bake at 425° about 10 min.
Variations: Use other flavorings. Add chocolate or butterscotch chips, cocoanut, nuts, grated orange or lemon rind to batter, or add 1½ tsp. anise seeds. Frostings and decorations may be used as on regular sugar cookies. Nutmeg may be omitted; other spices added.

CHERRY ROLL (eggless)

An excellent refrigerator cookie with many variations.

Cream together well ½ c. soft butter or margarine, ¾ c. sifted and packed powdered sugar.

Add and mix in ¼ tsp. vanilla, 1 tsp. half-and-half or milk

Stir in, in 2–3 additions 1¼ c. cake flour, ⅛ tsp. salt mixing until smooth each time.

Pat dough out on heavy waxed paper to ½-inch thickness. Sprinkle with ¼ c. candied cherries cut into eighths. Roll up like jelly roll to distribute cherries. It should be about 8 × 1½ inches. Wrap tightly in waxed paper and chill in refrigerator. It is easiest to cut if not too hard. Using a sawlike motion, cut with a sharp knife into thin slices—about ⅛ inch thick. Place on greased cookie sheet, chill in refrigerator until very firm before baking. Bake at 400° 7–8 min. or until golden brown. Do not overcook. Cool on cookie sheet about 1 min., then remove to cooling rack, gently. Yield: 3 doz.

Variations: Omit cherries. Substitute ½ tsp. orange extract and 1 T. grated orange rind; ½ tsp. lemon extract and grated lemon rind; ¼ c. *finely* chopped nuts and almond flavoring; ¼ c. *finely* cut cocoanut.

Chocolate Ribbon Pin Wheels: When mixing dough decrease milk to ½ tsp. and flour to 1 c. Divide dough in half. Pat first ½ onto waxed paper. To remaining half add ¼ c. cocoa and ½–1 tsp. more milk. Mix in. Pat out separately to same size as first half. Lift chocolate layer onto plain layer using the waxed paper to do so. Roll as a jelly roll. Having the chocolate layer inside makes rolling and cutting easier. *Variation:* Use peppermint flavoring.

BROWN SUGAR ICE BOX COOKIES (eggless)

Delicious for any occasion.

Cream 2 squares (½ lb.) room temp. butter with ½ c. sifted and packed brown sugar

Add and mix well 2 c. unsifted flour, ½ c. chopped nuts (optional)

Place on lightly floured dusted waxed paper. Lightly flour hands and make a roll about 1½ inches in diameter. Roll tightly in waxed paper. Chill thoroughly. It will keep several days in refrigerator. When ready to bake slice chilled roll into ¼-inch slices. Bake at 375° about 10 min. Yield: about 3 doz.

FRUIT FILLINGS FOR COOKIES, PASTRIES, ETC.

(eggless and milkless and gluten free)

Cook the following fillings over low heat until thick, 5–10 min., stirring occasionally.

Date and Date Nut	3 c. chopped dates or 2½ c. date chips, ¼ c. sugar, dash of salt, 1 T. grated orange rind, 1½ c. liquid—water, juice or sweet wine, ½ c. chopped nuts (optional)
Date Apricot	1 c. dates or chips, 2 c. chopped dried apricots, ½ c. sugar or to taste, 2 t. lemon juice, 1½–2 c. water
Raisin	2 c. seedless raisins, 1 c. +2 t. sugar, 1 tsp. cornstarch, ½ c. hot water. Add after thickened, 1 T. butter or shortening.
Prune Orange	3 c. chopped prunes, 2 T. grated orange rind, ½ c. each sugar and orange juice, 2 T. lemon juice.
Raisin, Fig and Date	1½ c. fruits in any proportion, ½ c. sugar, ½ c. water, and 2 T. lemon juice.
Pineapple Filling	Combine 1 c. sugar and 2 T. cornstarch. Stir in 1 No. 2 can drained crushed pineapple (1½ c.) 4 T. lemon juice, 3 T. margarine or shortening, ¼ tsp, nutmeg, ¾ c. pineapple juice.

Apricot Filling Combine 1¼ c. sugar, 1½ T. cornstarch. Stir in 2¼ c. chopped dried apricots, 1¼ c. water, ⅛ tsp. salt.

Uncooked Fillings Uncooked Fillings

Apple Filling Mix together and spread on prepared dough: ½ c. finely chopped apple, 3 T. soft raisins, 4 T. chopped nuts (optional), ¼ c. brown sugar, ½ tsp. cinnamon, 1½ T. melted butter or shortening.

Mincemeat; Jams and Marmalades, Chocolate or butterscotch morsels. See also page 34.

CRANBERRY COCOANUT BARS
(eggless and milkless)

Combine in bowl ½ c. flour, ¾ c. sifted, packed brown sugar dash of salt

Cut in ⅓ c. margarine or vegetable shortening

Mix in 1 c. quick cooking oats, ½ c. shredded cocoanut

Put ½ of mixture in well-greased 8 × 8-inch pan

Break up with fork 1 c. whole cranberry sauce. Pour off any excess liquid. Add 2 tsp. lemon juice.

Spread over cookie mixture. Pat remaining cookie mix over cranberry sauce. Bake at 350° about 40 min. Put on cooling rack. Cut into small squares for cookies, or large squares if it is to be served with whipped or ice cream. Good warm or cold.

RAISIN CRISPS (eggless and milkless)

Cover 1 c. seedless raisins with water and gently boil until raisins are soft. Drain off water. Add water to make ½ c. if necessary.

Cream well 1 c. shortening. Add gradually 1½ c. sugar

Sift together   3 c. sifted flour, 1 tsp. soda, 1 tsp. each cinnamon and nutmeg, ¼ tsp. cloves, ½ tsp. salt
Add alternately with raisin water. Stir in raisins.
Drop by teaspoonfuls onto ungreased cookie sheet. Bake at 375°
12–18 min. or until lightly browned. Yield: about 5 doz. medium.

SUGAR ROLL COOKIES (eggless)

A bit different and very good.
Soften   1 pkg. dry yeast in ½ c. warm water
Cream well   1 c. soft margarine, ¼ c. sugar. Add 1½ tsp.
vanilla
Sift together 2¼ c. sifted flour, 1½ tsp. baking powder, ½ tsp.
salt
Add yeast and flour to margarine.
The dough will be very soft. Using 2 tsp. shape balls and roll them
in plain sugar or cinnamon sugar. Place on greased cookie sheet.
Bake at 375° 20–25 min. Yield: 30 medium or 40 small cookies.
Variations: Add chopped candied fruits, chopped nuts, raisins, or
dates. Substitute other flavoring.

TEA CAKES

Tea Cakes No. 1 (milkless and eggless)
Measure 2 c. homemade pie crust mix. Add ½ c. sifted and packed
powdered sugar, ½–1 tsp. flavoring, ½–¾ c. chopped fruit or
nuts
Tea Cakes No. 2 (eggless)
Blend together 1 c. soft butter, ½ c. sifted packed powdered
sugar, ½–1 tsp. flavoring
Stir in   2¼ c. sifted cake flour or 2 c. all-purpose flour
¼ tsp. salt, fruit or nuts as above.
Method: Press the dough into balls a little smaller than a walnut.
Chill if too soft to handle. Place about 1 inch apart on ungreased

cookie sheet. Bake at 375° 10–15 min. or until firm but not brown. Roll in powdered sugar. Place on wire rack to cool.

Variations: Press into center of ball nut meats or candied fruit. Add to dough or roll after baking in shredded cocoanut or crushed cold cereal.

PUFF PASTE (eggless)

This delicate delicious pastry is not difficult but takes time because of the repeated chillings. It is easier if not done in one day. Yield: 4 doz. puffs.

Sift together in bowl 3½ c. flour, 1 tsp. salt

Cut in with pastry blender ¼ c. cold butter. Mixture should resemble coarse cornmeal

Add in small amounts 1–1¼ c. ice water.

Stir with fork and as the dough moistens push it aside so that you are always working with the undampened mix. Use only enough water to produce a dough moist enough to shape into a ball. Wrap tightly and chill thoroughly.

Cream 1¾ c. butter until soft and smooth; then chill.

When all is chilled divide dough in half for easier handling. On a floured pastry cloth roll into a very thin rectangle about ⅛ inch thick. Spread chilled butter evenly and gently over one layer. Cover with second layer and press all edges together. Lifting one side, fold towards middle until ⅓ of dough remains unfolded. Now fold that remaining ⅓ over the first fold. This makes 3 layers. Then fold the other direction the same way—1–2–3, to give you a small square 9 thicknesses deep and about 2 inches high. At no time should any butter come through a fold. Wrap tightly in waxed paper and chill.

On lightly floured pastry cloth straighten sides for easier rolling, then roll into thin rectangle as before. Be sure butter does not break through. Fold again as before, wrap and chill.

Repeat this process of rolling, folding, and chilling 3 more times. Be sure it is well wrapped each time. Up to this point the well-wrapped dough can remain in the refrigerator overnight, but if you can reach this stage in one day, it can remain refrigerated, *well wrapped,* for several days.

When ready to use, roll out once more on lightly floured pastry cloth to ¼–⅓-inch thickness. Cut into squares or rectangles and place well apart on a baking sheet which has been chilled with cold water and well drained. Prick with fork and chill. Bake at 450° for about 8 min. or until paste has puffed to about triple thickness; reduce heat to 350° and bake 10–20 min. or until lightly browned.

Store in tightly closed containers. They freeze well. To serve, sprinkle with powdered sugar, or slit with fork and fill with lemon or vanilla filling and top with melted semisweet chocolate to make Napoleons.

SIMPLIFIED PUFF PASTE (eggless)

Make recipe of plain pastry for two 9-inch crusts. Roll out. Dot with ⅓ c. butter. Roll up like jelly roll. Roll out into rectangle. Fold and seal. Wrap in waxed paper and chill.

To make pastry cups: Roll chilled dough to ⅛-inch thickness. Cut into circles large enough to fit backs of muffin tins or tart pans. Place very carefully so they do not overlap. Place on baking sheet. Chill again. Bake at 425° 20–30 min. Cover with brown paper after 15 min. to prevent excessive browning.

To make tart shells:

Roll pastry to ¼ inch thickness. Cut with biscuit cutter. Using a smaller cutter, cut out rings from center or enough to place two rings on top of each solid circle, binding them together with a *little* water. Bake as above 30–40 min. Cool and fill as desired or place carefully in an airtight container and freeze for later use.

BAKED PUDDINGS, UPSIDE DOWN CAKES, AND COBBLERS

BAKED PUMPKIN PUDDING (eggless)

This pudding is delicious and also makes an excellent pie filling.

Combine   1 lb. can or 2 c. pumpkin, ½ c. sugar, ¼ c. chopped
               nuts, 1 T. raisins or chopped dates in large bowl
Melt   2 T. margarine in heavy saucepan
Stir in, brown, but do not burn 2 T. flour
Add   1½ c. milk slowly, stirring, cooking slowly until
               thickened
Combine   ½ c. sugar, 1 tsp. cinnamon, ¼ tsp. salt, ¼ tsp.
               vanilla

Add to the sauce. Blend half of the sauce into the pumpkin
mixture, blending well. Pour into 1½ qt. buttered casserole. Pour
remaining sauce over top. Sprinkle with ¼ c. chopped nuts, and
1 T. more raisins or dates. Bake at 350° 40 min. Serve warm or
cold. Yield: 6–8 servings.

SPICED BREAD PUDDING (eggless)

Surprisingly good.

Combine   1½ c. toasted bread cubes (about 4 slices), 1 c.
               brown sugar, firmly packed, 1 tsp. soda, ½ tsp.
               nutmeg, ¼ tsp. ground cloves, 1 T. cinnamon, 1 c.
               raisins or date chips in large bowl
Stir in   1 c. buttermilk. Mix well.

Pour into greased 1½ qt. casserole. Bake at 350° 25–30 min.,
or until top is crisp and brown. Serve with half-and-half or cream.
4–5 servings.

CHOCOLATE BREAD PUDDING (eggless)

Using recipe above, substitute 3 T. cocoa for the spices, add
½ tsp. vanilla, use ½ c. drained chopped maraschino cherries
for raisins. Chopped nuts are optional.

COBBLERS

Cobblers are made with either enriched biscuit dough or cake
mix. Add 1–2 T. shortening and 2–3 T. sugar to regular biscuit mix.

EASY FRUIT COBBLER (eggless)

Mix   1 c. flour, 1½ tsp. baking powder, ⅓ c. sugar.
Cut in   3 T. shortening
Add ½ c. milk, or enough to make a soft dough. Roll to fit top of casserole or baking dish.

Use fresh, frozen, or canned fruit. Sweeten and thicken with sugar and cornstarch, amounts depending on the fruit. (1–2 T. cornstarch per cup of canned juice.) Flavoring extract optional. Cover fruit with dough, bake at 350–375° for 40–55 min. Cold fruit takes longer. For cake cobbler cover fruit with eggless cake batter.

DUMPLING PUDDING (eggless)

Quick, easy and good!

RAISIN OR DATE DUMPLING PUDDING (eggless)

Mix in pan   ½ c. firmly packed brown sugar, 1 c. water, 2 T.
              margarine
Boil 2 min. Add ½ tsp. vanilla. Keep hot while mixing batter
Combine   1 c. sifted flour, ½ c. sugar, 1½ tsp. baking powder,
              ¼ tsp. salt in a bowl
Add   ½ c. nuts (optional), ½ c. raisins or chopped dates, ½ c. milk, 2 T. melted margarine, ½ tsp. vanilla or almond extract. Beat vigorously. The batter will be thick. Pour hot syrup into an 8 × 8-inch pan or casserole. Over the hot syrup drop large spoonfuls of batter. Bake at 400° about 25 min. Best served warm.

Variations: Omit raisins or dates. Use ½ c. sliced drained maraschino cherries, add 2 T. cocoa to flour and use cherries and nuts. Make chocolate dumplings but use 1 c. strong coffee for water in the sauce. For more sauce, double syrup proportions and use deeper container.

BUTTERSCOTCH DUMPLINGS (eggless)

Very rich, delicious, easy and unusual.

Put 1 (1 lb.) pkg. brown sugar in heavy frying pan or skillet with a tight-fitting lid. Add about ¾ c. liquid—water, fruit juice, or coffee—and heat until bubbling. Make dumpling batter from commercial mix or add to your own mix 1 T. sugar and enough extra milk to make a batter to be dropped from a spoon (about 2 T. per 2 c.).

Spoon batter by tablespoons into gently bubbling sugar mixture. Cook uncovered 10 min. Then cover tightly and cook 10 min. longer. Do not lift the cover during this 10 min. Serve hot—plain, with half-and-half, whipped, or ice cream. Caution: If stove temperature is too high sugar will burn and the dumplings will be ruined.

Variation: Fruit may be added to syrup. Drop batter onto fruit.

HOT FUDGE PUDDING (eggless)

The sauce starts on top but goes to the bottom. Serve upside down.

Combine in bowl   1 c. sifted flour, 1¾ tsp. baking powder, ¼ tsp. salt, 1½ T. cocoa, ¾ c. sugar

Stir, mix well   ½ c. milk, 2 T. margarine, melted, 1 tsp. vanilla

Blend in   1 c. chopped nuts (optional)

Pour into well greased 8 × 8 × 2½-inch pan

Mix together   1 c. packed brown sugar, 4 T. cocoa. Sprinkle over batter

Pour gently over all 1⅓ to 2 c. hot water.

Bake at 350° 45 min. Invert servings so sauce is on top.

Variations: Mocha Pudding. Substitute 1 oz. chocolate melted with 2 T. butter for the cocoa in the sauce and 1½ c. strong coffee for the water.

USES FOR COMMERCIAL CAKE MIXES

CHOCOLATE PUDDING CAKE
(eggless)

Make one recipe (using 2 c. milk) of chocolate cornstarch pudding, either homemade or an eggless commercial mix.
Make 1 chocolate cake from mix (see page 43). Pour into ungreased oblong cake pan and pour hot pudding over batter.
Bake 35–40 min. at 350° for metal or 325° for glass.
The pudding goes to bottom for sauce. Serve upside down, warm.

CHERRY PUDDING CAKE
(eggless)

Thicken one No. 303 can (16 oz.) pie cherries with 1 c. sugar and 2 T. cornstarch. Add 1 tsp. red coloring, 2 T. melted margarine, ¾ tsp. almond extract.
Make white or yellow cake as above. Pour into greased and floured 12 × 9 × 2-inch pan or 3 qt. casserole.
Pour cherries gently over cake batter, pouring over a large spoon to avoid making holes in cake. Bake at 350° 50–60 min. or until cake tests done with toothpick.
Serve warm. It can be reheated at moderate temperature.
Variations: Blueberry Pudding Cake. Mix ½–¾ c. sugar, ⅔ T. cornstarch, ¼ tsp. nutmeg together. Use 2 cans blueberries with juice, 1–2 tsp. lemon juice. Proceed as above. For fresh blueberries use 1 qt. fresh fruit with 1 c. sugar, 1–2 T. cornstarch, ¼ tsp. nutmeg, ½ c. water, 1–2 tsp. lemon juice.
Other fruits and different cake mixes can be used.

CAKE MIX FRUIT CRISP
(eggless)

Spread pie filling or fruit, thickened and flavored as above, in a casserole, allowing plenty of depth for baking. For No. 2½ tin fruit use round 9-inch or 13 × 8 × 2-inch casserole. Sprinkle ½ pkg. regular size cake mix of your choice over top of fruit—not too thick.

Drizzle evenly over top of mix ½ c. melted margarine. Bake at 350° 35–40 min. or until topping is lightly browned and bubbly. Serve warm, plain, or with cream.

BAKED FRUIT CRUNCH
(eggless)

Prepare fruit filling as above. It must be as thick as pie filling. For 2 c. fruit or 1 No. 2½ size tin use ½ pkg. cake mix. Cut into mix ¼ c. margarine. Spread about ½ of mixture in bottom of 8- or 9-inch pan, patting lightly ½ inch up outer sides. Spread cool filling onto mixture but not over the edge of mix. Sprinkle remaining mix over top of filling. Bake at 350° about 45 min. Best served warm with whipped skim milk, cream, or ice cream. Chopped nuts may be added to mix.

BAKED APPLE PUDDING
(eggless and milkless)

Bread is used instead of cake or pastry for this excellent dessert. The better the bread, the better the results. (Use milkless where necessary.) Try homemade orange, cinnamon and raisin, or nut bread.

Use a 6- or 7 × 2½-inch or a 5 × 9 × 2½-inch casserole or pan. Cut enough bread into squares or fancy shapes to fit bottom and sides of container and enough extra for the top—12–18 slices, depending on waste from cutting. Dip bread into melted margarine or shortening and fit into casserole.

Fill this with very thick seasoned applesauce. (Canned sauce can be seasoned and cooked down to thicken.) Flavor sauce with lemon juice, brown sugar, honey, maple syrup, apricot preserves or orange marmalade. Spices such as cinnamon and nutmeg are also good.

Pour into casserole, cover with remaining bread, and bake on low rack of oven at 350–375° 45–55 min., or until lightly browned.

Let cool about 20 min. Invert onto serving dish. Serve warm with vanilla, rum or hard sauce.

SKILLET BERRY PUDDING WITH VARIATIONS
(milkless and eggless)

Made on top of the stove; quick easy and good.

Melt in frying pan	¼ c. margarine or vegetable shortening
Add and brown lightly	2–3 slices white bread cut in cubes. (1 c. bread cubes) (Use milkless bread where necessary)
Sprinkle in	¼ c. sugar, ½ tsp. cinnamon, ¼ tsp. nutmeg optional. Stir until dissolved
Stir in	1 can berry pie filling. Heat through.
Sprinkle with	2 T. sliced almonds (optional).

Serve warm (3–4 servings)

Variations: Use cherry or apple pie filling. Use 2 c. fresh or frozen fruit (packed without juice).

FRUIT CRISP TOPPINGS

No. 1:   Combine   1 c. white or brown sugar, ¾ c. flour 6 T. margarine. Cut in as for pie crust or melt and stir in.

No. 2:   Combine   ⅓ c. flour, ½ c. brown sugar, ¼ tsp. salt, cinnamon or nutmeg (optional), 1 c. uncooked oats.

Add and mix until crumbly: ½ c. melted margarine or shortening.

No. 3:   Combine   1 c. graham cracker crumbs, 1 T. flour, 1 c. brown sugar, ¼ tsp. salt, cinnamon and nutmeg (optional).

Stir in   ½ c. melted margarine or shortening.

No. 4:   Crumble cold cereal flakes to make 1½ c. and substitute for cracker crumbs.

No. 5:   For eggless, milkless and gluten free crisp, use gluten free cereal flakes, rice flour for wheat flour in No. 4.

Pat topping onto fruit, bake at 350° until fruit is cooked.

STEAMED PUDDINGS

All steamed puddings should be cooked in well greased covered molds—coffee cans, shortening cans, or fancy commercial pudding molds. Cover tightly with own lid or with tied wax paper. Place mold or molds on rack in large pan with enough water to steam the time indicated. Cover pan tightly, turn heat just high enough to maintain steaming. If using pressure cooker, follow accompanying directions.

ORANGE MARMALADE PUDDING
(eggless)

Unusually good.

Pour	1 c. milk over 3 c. *fine* soft breadcrumbs (5–6 slices)
Add	½ c. melted shortening
Blend in	¼ c. firmly packed brown sugar, ½ c. orange marmalade (one with lots of rind), ½ tsp. brandy flavoring
Mix well and add	1 c. sifted flour, 1 tsp. soda, 1 tsp. salt, 2½ tsp. pumpkin pie spice mix or 1 tsp. cinnamon, ¾ tsp. nutmeg, ¼ tsp. cloves, and ½ tsp. ginger
Add	½ c. chopped dates and ½ c. chopped nuts.

Steam in 1½ qt. mold (see above) 3 hrs. Serve hot with fruit or vanilla sauce or flame with sugar lumps soaked in orange or lemon extract.

FIG NEWTON STEAMED PUDDING
(eggless)

Use eggless fig newtons. This is delicious, reheats nicely, and freezes well.

Break up 2½ pkgs. (7¾ oz. each), a generous quart of fig newtons. Use fresh cookies. Pour 1 c. milk over cookies and let stand until cookies are mushy—about 15 min.

Sift together and blend well ½ c. sifted flour, 1 tsp. each soda and
cinnamon, ⅛ tsp. salt, ¼ tsp. ground cloves

Add   ¼ c. molasses, 1 T. lemon juice

Mix in completely   ½ c. melted margarine

Pour into 1½ qt. prepared mold. Steam about 3 hrs. Serve hot with sauce of choice.

AMBROSIAL CARROT PUDDING
(eggless and milkless)

The texture of this pudding is so feathery light it is hard to believe the basic ingredients are those of other steamed puddings. By varying the fruit it becomes an all-winter dessert, or a festive holiday pudding.

Mix together   1 c. ground dry bread crumbs, 1 c. brown sugar
1 tsp. each salt, soda, cinnamon, nutmeg, and allspice

Mix together   1 c. ground carrots, 1 c. ground raw potatoes, 1 c. chopped dates or date chips, 2 c. glazed fruit mixture or mixture of raisins, currants, dates and nuts.

Cut into carrot mixture ½ c. margarine or vegetable shortening.
Combine two mixtures well. Fill mold ⅔ full. Cover tightly and steam 3 hrs. Serve with lemon, brandy or fruit sauce.

PIE CRUSTS

Good pie crust need not be difficult if certain precautions are taken in the making. Measurements should be accurate to insure the right proportion of flour to shortening. Too much shortening does not make a more flaky crust, but one that is greasy, crumbly, and hard to handle. Too little makes a hard, tough crust. Using part lemon juice in the ice water seems to give a more tender crust, and it is true that when treated like puff paste extra flakiness can be obtained.

The temperature of the shortening also affects the texture of the crust. Cold shortening gives a more flaky product but it is not as tender as with room temperature shortening.

Too much water and too much handling will make an inferior crust no matter what the flour and shortening relationship. Use as little ice water as possible to hold the crust together. Handle as little as possible. Using a pastry cloth and cover for the rolling pin cuts down the amount of flour needed as well as the amount of handling. A thin crust will be flakier than a thick one.

Roll the crust large enough to fit loosely into the pie tin. A stretched crust will shrink in the baking. Prick an empty pie shell well to prevent puffing during baking. Bake carefully 7–10 min. at 425° or until pale golden brown.

There are good pie crust mixes available but they give a less flaky crust than homemade, are more expensive, and about the same amount of work as using a homemade mix made in large quantity. This mix (recipe below) keeps well, if tightly covered, and can be made in larger amounts if desired. A variety of other crusts are also given.

HOMEMADE PASTRY MIX
(eggless and milkless)

In a large bowl mix   6 c. flour, 1 T. salt

Cut in with knives or pastry blender 2 c. shortening

Mixture should be like cornmeal with some chunks in it. Keep in tightly covered container and use as needed. It keeps well unrefrigerated in normal moderate temperatures.

For a 2-crust 9-inch pie, or 2 9-inch shells:

Measure into bowl   2⅓ c. pastry mix
Stir in gradually   3–4 T. ice water

Use just enough so mixture will hold together. Divide in half. Shape with hands into balls. On lightly floured pastry cloth roll out to fit pie tin.

Variations:

Use lemon or orange juice for liquid plus ½ tsp grated orange rind.

Nut crust. Add ¼ c. ground nuts—almonds, hazel nuts, brazil nuts, or walnuts. These are especially good with a cream nut filling.

Sesame seed crust. Add ½ c. toasted sesame seeds to the flour. Proceed as for regular crust. Especially good with baked pumpkin pie.

Seasoned crust. Add 1 tsp. cinnamon or nutmeg, or combination of two to flour. Good for fruit pies.

EXTRA-RICH PASTRY

Roll regular pastry to ⅛-inch thickness. Dot with 1 T. firm but not hard butter. Fold so outside edges meet in center. The pastry will be half the original width but the same length. Seal edges. Fold long ends to center and seal. Re-roll to fit pan. Proceed as above. Bake about 8 min. at 475°.

OATMEAL CRUST
(eggless and milkless)

Mix together   ¾ c. sifted flour, ½ c. oats, ½ tsp. salt
Cut in   ⅓ c. vegetable shortening
Add   3–4 T. ice water

Proceed as for plain crust. Bake at 450° 10–12 min.

CRUMB CRUSTS
(eggless and gluten free)

For 9-inch pie

Measure   1⅓ c. crumbs (chocolate, vanilla, or ginger snap egg-
          less cookies, or graham crackers or zwieback crumbs
          plus ¼ c. sugar). For gluten free use gluten free dry
          cereal

Stir in   ⅓ c. melted butter or margarine.

Mix well. Pat firmly and evenly into pie pan covering both
bottom and sides. Either bake or chill. Baking gives a firmer
crust. Bake at 325° 8–10 min. or until firm. For unbaked, chill
several hours.

CHOCOLATE COCOANUT PIE SHELL
(eggless and gluten free)

Melt over boiling water   2 T. margarine, 2 squares bitter choc-
                          olate

Mix together   2 T. hot milk, ⅔ c. firmly packed
                          powdered sugar. Combine the two
                          mixtures and stir well.

Put into bowl   1½ c. moist shredded cocoanut.

Add chocolate mixture and mix well. Put into pie tin as a crumb
crust. Chill until firm.

Variation: Plain cocoanut crust. Use 1 T. additional margarine
instead of chocolate.

COOKIE-TEXTURED PIE CRUST

See Pie Cake tartlets, p. 47.

TWO-CRUST PIES

Fruit pies are seldom problems for eggless or milkless cooking.
Substitutions can also be made for gluten free pies. Only a few less
common recipes are included here. Helpful hints for two-crust pies:
Sprinkle 1 tsp. dry white bread crumbs in bottom of crust before
putting in filling. (Lessens chance of sogginess.) Have top crust
ready to place immediately filling is in. Put in oven as quickly as
possible.

FRESH PLUM PIE
(eggless, milkless, and gluten free)*

A tangy midsummer pie from Nubiana, Santa Rose, or Wickham plums for that in-between fruit season. Prepare pastry for 9-inch two-crust pie, regular or gluten free.

Peel, pit and slice   3½–4 c. tart plums

Add   1¼ T. lemon juice, ½ tsp. grated rind

Mix in bowl   1–1½ c. sugar (half brown and half white) depending on sweetness of fruit; ¼ c. flour, ¼ tsp. each nutmeg, cinnamon, ⅛ tsp. salt.

Add sugar mixture to plums and stir until well blended. Pour into prepared crust. Dot with margarine (omit for milkless). Cover with top crust. Seal edges well. Sprinkle with sugar. Bake at 450° 10 min., then reduce temperature to 350° and bake 30 min. more.

PINEAPPLE CARAMEL PIE
(eggless, milkless and gluten free)**

Prepare crust. Use either a lattice or full top crust.

Combine in pan   ¾ c. brown sugar, 3 T. cornstarch, ¼ tsp. salt

Blend in gradually   1 No. 2½ size can crushed pineapple

Cook, stirring constantly, until mixture is thick and clear

Stir in   1 T. grated lemon or orange peel, 2 T. margarine or vegetable shortening.

Cool mixture until it has stopped steaming or bottom crust will be soggy. Fill crust, cover, and bake at 425° 30–35 min.

---

* Use gluten free pie crust (see page 120). Substitute 2 T. cornstarch for flour.

** Use gluten free pie crust (see page 120).

MYSTERY PIE
(eggless, milkless and gluten free)*

The tantalizing flavor of this tropical pie is completely challenging. Different and delicious.

Prepare pastry for 9-inch pie. Line pan.

Steam in sieve over hot water, 2 c. date chips, or use 2 c. chopped date.

Peel all skin and membrane from 2 large or 3 small lemons.

Slice VERY thin, removing all seeds.

Mix together ½ c. flour, 2 c. sugar. Sprinkle a layer of sugar-flour on crust. Cover with lemon slices and then a layer of dates. Repeat—sugar-flour, lemon and dates, ending with layer of lemon slices and any remaining sugar-flour. Sprinkle with water—up to ¼ c. if lemons are not really juicy. Cover with top crust. Seal edges tightly. Sprinkle with a little sugar. Bake at 400° 40–45 min. This is a filling pie, so start with small servings. 6–8 servings.

CREAM PIES

With the adaptations given below, these recipes are varied, delicious, and missing much hidden fat and many calories normally found in cream pies. All are eggless, a few milkless, and many gluten free with the use of gluten free crust and flour substitutions.

WHIPPED EVAPORATED MILK FOR PIES

Chill milk in refrigerator tray or shallow pan until half frozen. Pour into well-chilled bowl. Use chilled beaters. Whip at high speed until partly whipped. Then add 3 T. instant dry milk for each ½–⅔ c. milk. Continue beating until very stiff. Use immediately.

---

* Use gluten free pie crust. See page 120. Substitute ¼ c. cornstarch for flour.

GRASSHOPPER PIE
(eggless and gluten free)

Guaranteed to bring forth compliments.

Melt over low heat   2 c. miniature marshmallows, ⅓ c. milk or half-and-half

Stir to prevent sticking or burning.

Cool and add   3 drops oil of peppermint, a few drops green color

Chill until it begins to hold its shape.

Fold in   1 small can evaporated milk whipped according to directions above

Pile into prepared baked crust, regular or gluten free.

To give a special touch, melt ½ c. semisweet chocolate chips with one or two T. water and pour over top of pie; or sprinkle top with shaved chocolate. Chill until set.

Variation: Chocolate Mint Pie—Omit food coloring, melt ½ c. chocolate chips with marshmallows and milk.

LEMON FLUFF PUDDING OR PIE FILLING
(eggless and gluten free)

Light and lemony, a good substitute for conventional lemon pie filling. Use plain or in choice of crusts, regular or gluten free.

Mix together in pan   ½ c. sugar, 1 envelope plain gelatin, dash of salt

Stir in   ½ c. cold water

Let stand 3–5 min., place over low heat, stir until gelatin and sugar dissolved.

Remove from heat, cool slightly.

Stir in   1 (6 oz.) can undiluted frozen lemonade

Blend well. Chill until mixture forms a mound when dropped from a spoon. It must not be runny.

Fold into   1 small can evaporated milk, whipped according to directions above.

Pile into 9-inch crust or pudding dish. Chill until set.

LEMON CREAM PIE
(eggless and gluten free)

Unbelievably good without eggs.

Combine and mix well   1½ c. sugar, 7 T. cornstarch, ½ tsp. salt

Slowly add   1½ c. boiling water

Cook, stirring constantly, until thick and smooth.

Stir in   3 T. margarine, ½ c. lemon juice, fresh or undiluted frozen, 1 tsp. grated rind, yellow food coloring (optional)

Take out 1 c. full and set aside for glaze.

Soften   1 tsp. plain gelatin ¼ c. cold water

Heat until melted; add to remaining lemon mixture.

Stir in   ½ c. evaporated milk, ½ c. half-and-half

Stir until cooled, pour into prepared baked crust (9-inch), regular or gluten free; cover top with the 1 c. glaze. Chill thoroughly.

GRAHAM CRACKER APPLESAUCE PIE
(eggless, milkless, and gluten free)*

A quick and easy version of apple pie.

Make a graham cracker crust. Cut cool crust into desired size servings, place carefully on serving plates. Top with warm or cold well-seasoned thick applesauce. Top with whipped cream, ice cream, or cinnamon sauce.

PUMPKIN CHIFFON PIE
(eggless and gluten free)

Dissolve   2 tsp. plain gelatin in ¼ c. cold water

---

* Use gluten free cereal crust. For milkless use oatmeal crust.

Mix together in pan   1 c. packed brown sugar, 2 T. cornstarch,
                      ½ tsp. each salt, ginger and allspice, 2 tsp.
                      cinnamon, 1⅓ c. pumpkin
Add   ¾ c. milk.

Cook about 10 min. or until mixture is thick and cornstarch is
cooked. Add gelatin, stir until it is dissolved. Cool mixture until
it begins to set. Fold in 1 small can (⅔ c.) evaporated milk
whipped as directed above. Turn into baked 9-inch crust, regular
or gluten free. Chill.

BAKED PUMPKIN PIE
(eggless and gluten free)*

In a bowl combine   1 c. packed brown sugar, 2 T. cornstarch,
                    2 T. flour, ½ tsp. salt, 1 tsp. pumpkin pie
                    spice mix (or your own mix), 2 c. pumpkin
Mix well; blend in   1½ c. milk (part half-and-half or orange
                    juice optional), 1 tsp. vanilla.

Pour into 9-inch unbaked pie shell, regular or gluten free, bake at
450° for 10 min. Reduce temperature to 325°. Bake 35 min.
longer or until knife inserted in center comes out clean. Cool on
cookie rack.

BUTTERSCOTCH PIE
(eggless and gluten free)

Exceptionally good! Either butter or margarine can be used
but butter gives a better flavor.

In 1½ qt. pan mix   2 T. cornstarch, 3 T. sugar, ½ tsp. salt,
                    1 tsp. unflavored gelatin
Stir in slowly   1⅔ c. cold milk. No lumps please.
Set aside.

In a heavy 1 qt. pan heat over medium heat
                    6 T. butter until golden brown (don't burn
                    it)

---

* Omit flour and use 1 more T. cornstarch.

Add   1 c. firmly packed dark-brown sugar
Stir in   ½ c. water. Boil 2–3 min., stirring con-
                   stantly.

Remove from heat, add to milk mixture. Cook over medium heat until thick and the cornstarch is thoroughly cooked—10 min. or more. Stir constantly to avoid sticking. It will not hold its shape when done, but the gelatin will set it. Stir in 1 tsp. vanilla. Continue stirring until it stops steaming and is cool enough to put into baked 9-inch shell, regular or gluten free.

SHOO-FLY PIE WITH VARIATIONS
(eggless and milkless)

Measure and mix until crumblike   1 c. flour, ¾ c. brown sugar,
                                  ⅓ c. margarine, butter, or
                                  vegetable shortening for milk-
                                  less.

Sprinkle half of it into greased pie plate or into unbaked pie shell.

Combine   ½ c. sorghum or dark corn syrup, 1 c. water, ½
             generous tsp. soda, then add 1 tsp. vinegar.

Pour mixture onto a spoon over crumb mixture to spread evenly. Sprinkle with rest of crumbs. Bake at 450° 15 min., then 25–30 min. at 325° or until crust and top are well browned. Remove to cake rack to cool several hours before cutting. Serves 6–8.

Variations: Pecan Pie: Mix 1 c. chopped pecans into crumb mixture. Surprisingly like caramel pecan pie.

Date or Date nut: Add 1 c. chopped dates or dates and nuts.

Raisin or Raisin nut: Substitute raisins for dates.

CREAM PIES WITH CORNSTARCH PUDDING BASE
(eggless and gluten free)

The basis of these eggless cream pies is cornstarch pudding. It can be as rich as your fat allowance permits or as you desire, but it can still give excellent results and remain low-fat. The numerous variations possible make this recipe important.

BASIC CORNSTARCH PUDDING

Combine in pan   4 T. cornstarch, 4 T. sugar, ⅛ tsp. salt, 1 tsp.
                  gelatin, (for pie only)
Measure   2 c. milk or cream.

Pour a small amount of the cold milk over the cornstarch mixture and stir until perfectly smooth to make a thin paste. Let this stand several min. while remainder of milk is heated; add hot milk slowly to cornstarch mixture and cook over medium heat, stirring constantly until it is thick and smooth and cornstarch is thoroughly cooked. Where gelatin is omitted, the whole amount of milk can be stirred in slowly at one time and cooked immediately.

Stir in   1 tsp. vanilla or other flavoring, 1 T. butter.

For pudding pour directly into serving dishes or bowl. Serve warm or cold, plain, or with sauce or cream.

For pie, stir until cool, add variation as desired or suggested, and pour into prepared baked shell, regular or gluten free.

Variations: Omit vanilla. Use different flavorings: almond, orange, or lemon with grated rind, peppermint, rum or rum and coffee (1–2 tsp. instant added to dry ingredients); add sliced bananas or banana flakes, 1 c. chopped raisins, dates, nuts or fruit and nuts, mincemeat, chopped prunes, cocoanut, alone or with chocolate.

For chocolate, add 2 T. cocoa to dry ingredients, 2 squares shaved bitter chocolate to hot milk; or chocolate with banana or nuts.

Fudge topping: Mix ½ c. sifted powdered sugar, ⅛ tsp. salt, 2 T. cream. Blend in 1 oz. melted bitter chocolate and 2 T. butter. Spread on filling just before serving. Also good on baked pumpkin pie.

For glazes, see fresh fruit pies.

CHIFFON CREAM PIES

To make chiffon cream pies of any of the above, add a small can evaporated milk whipped or whipped cream to pudding. This lightens the texture but dilutes the flavor, so adjust accordingly. Cocoa may be added to evaporated milk when partly whipped.

CHIFFON FRUIT PIES
(eggless and gluten free)

ORANGE CHIFFON PIE

Mix in small pan 2 tsp. plain gelatin, ⅓ c. orange juice.

Let sit until dissolved, then heat until melted.

Add, depending on sweetness of juice ½–¾ c. sugar. Stir until melted. Add sugar gelatin mixture to 1 c. more orange juice, 1 T. grated rind. Set in refrigerator until mixture just holds shape. It should not be stiff.

Fold gently into 1 small can evaporated milk whipped (see page 71).

Pile gently into prepared crust. Chill in refrigerator several hours or until completely set before using. Garnish with very thin slices or sections of oranges, or mandarins.

Variations: Omit orange juice. Use grapefruit juice and 1–2 tsp. grated lemon peel for orange rind; use ⅔ c. lemon or lime juice and ⅔ c. water. Adjust sugar and use lemon rind; use 1 c. apricot nectar and ⅓ c. lemon juice; use 1 c. cranberry juice or melted jelly and ⅓ c. orange juice with 1 T. grated orange rind; to use whole cranberry sauce, heat it and strain out fruit. Use juice for liquid. Add orange juice or water if needed to make 1⅓ c. Add fruit with whipped milk. For prune chiffon substitute prune juice including 2 T. lemon juice. Decrease sugar to ½–⅓ c. Add ½ c. well-drained chopped prunes and ½ c. chopped nuts (optional).

Pineapple chiffon: Drain well 1 No. 303 can crushed pineapple. Measure juice and add enough more, or other juice or water to make 1½ c. Fold in drained pineapple with whipped milk.

ORANGE MARSHMALLOW CREAM
(eggless and gluten free)

To a 6 oz. can of concentrated frozen orange juice add enough water to make 1 c. Place in a pan with ¼ lb. marshmallows (about 16 large or ⅓ pkg. miniatures). Over low heat, stir until marshmallows are melted. Remove from heat and cool. Add 2 tsp. grated orange rind. When partially set fold in ½ c. evaporated milk whipped according to directions, page 71. Place in prepared pie shell, regular or gluten free. Chill well.

Variations: Berry Mallow: Substitute 1 c. berries and juice for orange juice. Omit rind. *Chocolate Mallow:* Use 1 c. milk or half-and-half with marshmallows. Add 2 squares shaved unsweetened chocolate and ⅛ tsp. salt. Cocoa can also be added to the whipped milk. *Butterscotch mallow:* Use ½ c. milk and ⅔ c. butterscotch sauce with marshmallows. Add ⅛ tsp. salt.

GLAZED FRESH FRUIT PIES
(eggless and gluten free)

These are delicious too and also offer great variety. Make a rich pastry, the crust given for pie cake tartlets, or gluten free crust. Use a pie tin, tart pan, or cake tin with removable bottom. Fill baked crust half-full with cream-pie filling flavored to complement the fruit you use, or use cream cheese filling (recipe below). Chill thoroughly. This much can be done a day ahead, but fruit should be added and glazed as near serving time as possible—not more than 2 hrs. before. Most any fresh fruit in season is good, or combinations are interesting. Place prepared fruit neatly over filling, glaze* lightly with pastry brush or spoon.

CREAM CHEESE FILLING

Beat until smooth and creamy	1 8-oz. pkg room temperature cream cheese
Add gradually and mix well	⅓ c. sieved and packed powdered sugar
Add and mix in	⅓ c. flavoring and half-and-half combined.

---

* See page 79.

The flavoring may be extract, liqueur or juice or frozen juice concentrate (thawed). Measure 2–3 T. liqueur or juice or ½–1 tsp. extract in measuring cup. Fill to ⅓ c. with half-and-half or cream.

Sample combinations: Vanilla filling with mixed raspberries and blueberries with raspberry glaze; orange curaçao-flavored filling with sliced fresh figs and thickened lemonade for glaze; cherry liqueur-flavored filling with cherries and peach jam glaze; peppermint filling with fresh pineapple and apricot-pineapple glaze; almond-flavored filling with sliced peaches or nectarines with cherry glaze.

GLAZES
(eggless, milkless, gluten free)

The easiest glazes are made by melting jelly, jam, or marmalade. Strain the latter two to make a clear glaze. Cool to lukewarm before brushing onto fruit, which should be cold.

To make glazes from fresh or fresh-frozen fruit, mash 1 pt. fruit, cover with ¾ c. sugar. Let stand 1 hr. Strain out seeds and solid fruit. If there is not 1½ c. juice add water to make that amount.

Bring juice to a boil. Mix ¼ c. sugar and 3 T. cornstarch. Stir enough boiling juice into sugar-cornstarch to make a thin paste. Pour paste into remaining juice slowly. Cook over low heat stirring constantly until it boils. Let boil 1 min. Cool. Spoon over chilled fruit in pie. Chill 1–2 hrs.

REFRIGERATOR AND FREEZER DESSERTS
(eggless and gluten free)

Some of the most gourmet desserts are found here—lovely icebox cakes as well as many frozen desserts. The "pound cake" recipe is the basis of many of these, but other cakes can be substituted as well as gluten free cakes for wheatless recipes. Much can be accomplished without eggs or whipped cream. Of course, whipped cream can be substituted for the evaporated milk, and sweetened whipped cream can be used as frosting instead of the filling given in the recipe, but whipped evaporated milk is used in the recipes below.

There are two methods, slightly different, for preparing whipped evaporated milk. Where a more fragile texture similar to whipped cream is desired, use Method No. 1. For a product that will have a firmer texture and freeze well use Method No. 2.

WHIPPED MILK METHOD NO. 1

Pour milk into shallow pan and place in freezer until partially frozen. Pour into well-chilled bowl and use cold beaters. Whip at high speed until partially set. Add 2 T. powdered nonfat milk per ½ c. evaporated milk. (Use 3 T. if lemon juice is not added, as follows.) Add 2 T. lemon juice if it will not detract from the flavor of the finished product, and ¼ c. sieved and packed powdered sugar. Whip gently until above are stirred in, then at high speed until milk is very stiff. Proceed according to recipe directions. Use quickly.

WHIPPED MILK METHOD NO. 2

Gelatin is added to the milk here to insure a firmer texture. A general rule is to use ¼ tsp. unflavored gelatin for each ½ c. evaporated milk.

Dissolve gelatin in 1 T. cold water. Let stand 5 min. Heat gently until melted. Very slowly add 1–2 T. evaporated milk, stirring to prevent lumping. If it does congeal, reheat and add more milk more slowly, then add to the remaining milk. Put into freezer. It will not freeze into crystals as the plain milk does but sets like gelatin. Remove to chilled bowl and proceed as for plain whipped milk.

This is used in many of the frozen desserts. If properly flavored there will be no canned milk flavor.

REFRIGERATOR CREAM CAKES
(eggless and gluten free)

The following six recipes all use eggless "pound cake" as the base. Other eggless cakes may be used, or gluten free but not eggless recipes (see Breads and Desserts) used for wheatless. Make 2–3 9-inch round layers. Refrigerate all finished cakes until serving time. Filling and frosting are best done the day they are to be used unless frozen. Do not serve frozen.

Fresh Orange Cream Cake: Use orange flavoring and add 1 tsp. grated rind to cake batter. Between cool layers of cake, spread ⅓ of following filling.

Mix together   1 c. sugar, ½ tsp. salt, 4 T. cornstarch.

Stir in slowly   1 c. orange juice and pulp.

Cook over moderate heat stirring until it thickens. Boil 1 min. Remove from heat. Blend in 1–2 T. grated orange rind, 1½ T. lemon juice, 2 T. butter or margarine. Cool. Spread ⅓ of filling on bottom layer of cake. Refrigerate to set.

Whip ½ c. evaporated milk by method No. 1 using lemon juice. Stir in remaining orange filling. Add more grated rind (optional). Frost cake. Garnish is optional. Grated chocolate or chocolate curls; or well-drained mandarin sections or orange slices added at serving time.

Variation: Divide filling between layers and the top. Use cream cheese icing for sides of cake.

Apricot Baba: Make two-layer "pound cake." Drain fruit from one No. 2½ tin canned apricots. Puree the pitted fruit. Add 2–3 T. rum extract. It takes this amount to give proper flavor. Spoon ½ apricot rum puree over bottom layer of warm cake. Let rest until cool. Place top layer. Shortly before serving time spread with apricot mousse (see recipe page 86) made with remaining half of puree which has been removed from freezer long enough to be spreadable. Refrigerate until ready to serve.

Wine Cream Cake: Sprinkle bottom layer of cake with 4–5 T.

loganberry, blackberry, or sherry wine. Sweeten 2 c. thick commercial half-and-half or regular sour cream with 1 c. powdered sugar. Spread half on bottom layer of cake. Blend one 3 oz. pkg. cream cheese into remaining sour cream and frost top layer. Chill thoroughly.

Variation: Liqueur may be used instead of wine.

Chocolate Cream Cake: Whip one large can or 1½ c. evaporated milk by method No. 1, omitting lemon juice, and add ½ c. cocoa. Spread this between layers and use as frosting.

Variations: Add 2–3 T. creme de cocoa to whipped milk. Use ¾ c. powdered nonfat milk. For chocolate mint: Add 2–3 drops oil of peppermint. Mocha: Pour 1 T. boiling water over 2 tsp. instant coffee. Add to milk before chilling.

Strawberry Cream Cake: Spread following mixture between layers and use also as frosting. Mash 1 pt. fresh or frozen strawberries. Add 2 T. sugar. Soften 1 tsp. plain gelatin in 1 T. of the juice. Dissolve over hot water. Stir gradually into remaining berries. Chill until partially set. Then fold into ½ c. evaporated milk whipped according to method No. 1.

Variation: Substitute other berries, apricots, peaches, etc.

Lemon Cream Cake: Use lemon cream pie filling, lemon cornstarch pudding, or lemon yogurt cream (recipe below) as filling for cake.

YOGURT SAUCES AND FILLINGS

Low-fat yogurt is a delicious and wonderful substitute for high-fat sour cream. It is available in many flavors, or the plain yogurt can be flavored to taste. Because yogurt is slightly tart it lends itself beautifully to citrus and other fruits, and can be sweetened to taste. Use as fruit sauce for other fruits, cakes or puddings, or eat unadorned.

To make sauces: Use 1 c. thick yogurt. Add 1 c. mashed or chopped fruit; 2–3 T. lemon juice; 3 T. undiluted frozen orange juice or grapefruit juice, or vanilla extract to taste. Add ½–1 c. sieved packed powdered sugar or to taste.

Filling: Lemon. To 1 c. plain yogurt add ¾ c. powdered sugar. Soften 1 tsp. plain gelatin in 1 T. lemon juice. Dissolve over hot water. Add 3 T. more lemon juice slowly, then stir in yogurt. Adjust sugar to taste. This will jell in the refrigerator so either put it on cake before completely set or jell in the same size pan as cake so it can be inverted over cake or slid onto it.

LEMON CHEESE CAKE
(eggless and gluten free)

Zwieback or graham cracker crust is especially good with this. Gluten free cookie crust can also be used. Make it for a pie tin or double recipe for cheese cake, and use a deeper casserole or pan with removable bottom.

Stir in bowl	1 8-oz. pkg. cream cheese until soft and creamy
Blend in	½ c. milk until creamy
Add	1½ c. milk, 1 pkg. lemon instant pudding
	1½ tsp. grated lemon rind, ⅓ tsp. lemon extract.

Beat gently until just mixed. Pour into prepared cooled crust. Chill thoroughly.

ORANGE YOGURT CHEESE CAKE
(eggless and gluten free)

Soften	1 tsp. gelatin in 1 T. orange juice
Dissolve over hot water	Add 3 T. more orange juice, stirring
To	1 c. thick yogurt add ½ c. sieved and packed powdered sugar and the orange juice.

If you have a blender, blend 1 c. fine-curd cottage cheese at high speed until the consistency of cream cheese, or use 1 8-oz. pkg. cream cheese stirred until creamy. Fold into yogurt mixture, adjust flavoring and pour into prepared crusts as above.

CHOCOLATE ICE CREAM PIE
(eggless and gluten free)

A delicious dessert to top off a light meal. Very rich.

In heavy pan   Melt 16 large marshmallows in ½ c. milk or half-and-half

Melt and add   7 small almond nut Hershey bars.

Refrigerate until partially set, add ½ pt. unwhipped heavy cream or 1 large can evaporated milk. Put into graham cracker or gluten free cereal crust. Freeze.

ICE CREAMS, SHERBETS, MOUSSES
(eggless and gluten free)

Good commercial eggless ice cream is not available. Mechanical freezers at home solve the problem and are so easy to use. Refrigerator ice creams have a different texture but are smooth and good if properly made.

GENERAL RECIPE FOR ELECTRIC FREEZERS

Scald   1 qt. cream (of desired fat content). The richer the cream, the richer the finished product.

Add   ⅔ c. sugar. Cool. Blend in 1½ T. vanilla, dash of salt.

Pour into freezer container, freeze according to freezer directions. Usually 4–5 parts crushed ice to one part rock salt recommended.

Yield: 1 qt.

Variations: These are endless. Adjust sugar accordingly.

Samples: Add 1 c. shaved semisweet chocolate; 1 c. ground or blended butterscotch chips; 1 c. peanut brittle (crushed); ½ c. crushed peppermint stick candy; 1 c. crushed lemon drops; 1 c. chopped nuts; ½ c. grapenuts; 2 T. instant coffee added to hot milk; 2½ squares chocolate melted in ¼ c. hot water; 1½ c.

mashed fruit; ½ c. orange juice and pulp plus 1 tsp. grated orange rind (or use undiluted frozen juice for stronger flavor).

REFRIGERATOR ICE CREAMS

Vanilla: Mix 2 T. cornstarch, ¼ tsp. salt, ¾ c. sugar
Scald   2 c. milk or half-and-half
Pour milk slowly over sugar mixture, stirring, and cook until thickened and cornstarch is cooked. Cool.
Add   1 T. vanilla.
 Fold into 1 large can (1⅓ c.) evaporated milk whipped according to method No. 1 (see page 80) but omitting sugar, or 1 c. heavy cream whipped. Put into freezer tray in refrigerator. Stir several times as it freezes. See variations for electric freezer ice cream above. Adjust proportions.

ELEGANT STRAWBERRY ICE CREAM

Boil together 5 min. 1 c. sugar, 1 c. water. Cool
Add   1 c. mashed strawberries, or other fruit
             1 T. lemon juice
Stir in   ¾ c. cream—as heavy as feasible. Whipping cream gives the best results.
Pour into freezer tray (or mechanical freezer). Stir several times during freezing.

LEMON ICE CREAM

Pour   2 c. milk over 1 c. sugar. Stir until dissolved
Add   1–2 tsp. grated lemon rind, about ⅓ c. lemon juice.
The mixture should be quite curdled. Freeze about 1 hr. or until mushy. Whip 1 small can evaporated milk by method No. 1 (see page 80) using 2 T. more lemon juice; or use ½ pt. whipping cream whipped. Add to first part mixing well; refreeze, stirring several times.

MOUSSE
(eggless and gluten free)

A very satisfactory substitute for commercial ice cream. 6–8 servings.

Whip: 1 large can evaporated milk by method No. 2. See page 80 (2 c. heavy cream whipped may be substituted.)

For *Peppermint Mousse,* add 4–5 drops oil of peppermint or ⅓ c. peppermint candy crushed and soaked in 1 T. half-and-half. Freeze. For candy, decrease sugar to ¼ c.

Chocolate: Add ½ c. cocoa.

Chocolate Peppermint: Add ½ c. cocoa to milk as above, and 4–5 drops oil of peppermint.

Pineapple and Pineapple Mint: Add 1 c. well drained crushed pineapple; for pineapple mint, add 2 drops oil of peppermint also.

Apricot Rum: Add 1 c. drained pureed apricots and 2 T. rum extract.

Fruit: Add fruit pulp of choice.

Burnt Almond: Heat, stirring constantly, until melted and golden brown ½ c. sugar. Add and simmer until sugar is entirely dissolved ½ c. boiling water. Use care—it sputters. Chill. Add whipped milk, 1 tsp. vanilla, and ¼ c. chopped roasted almonds. Substitute ½ tsp. almond extract for nuts (optional). Freeze.

MALLOWS
(eggless and gluten free)

ORANGE MARSHMALLOW CREAM

Follow directions for orange marshmallow cream pie. Instead of using as pie filling, freeze.

CHOCOLATE MALLOW

Add ½ c. water to ½ c. evaporated milk. Pour over ¼ c. cocoa making a smooth paste. Add ¼ lb. marshmallows. Steam until melted.

Add 1½ T. vanilla, ⅛ tsp. salt. When cold and partially set, fold in 1 c. evaporated milk whipped by method No. 1 but leaving out the sugar and lemon juice. Freeze. Serves 8.

BERRY MALLOW

Pour ½ c. milk over ½ lb. miniature marshmallows. Heat until melted. Let cool. Pour off juice from 1 No. 303 can of berries. Make a paste using part of the juice and 3 T. cornstarch. Heat remaining juice, add paste, and cook, stirring until mixture is thick and clear.

Stir in 1 T. lemon juice and berries. Combine with marshmallows and cool. Gently fold into berry mixture 1 small can whipped milk (method No. 1 omitting sugar) or 1 c. whipped cream. Freeze, or spread over graham cracker crumbs with more sprinkled on top and chill until set. 10–12 servings.

SHERBETS AND ICES
(eggless and gluten free)

These are smoother made in a mechanical freezer but can be surprisingly good in the refrigerator if stirred sufficiently.

APRICOT MILK SHERBET

Dissolve 1 c. sugar in 3 c. apricot nectar. Add 2 T. lemon juice, ½ tsp. almond extract. Stir in 2 c. half-and-half. Freeze. Stir several times.

Variation: Use any desired combination of fruit juices.

LEMON OR LEMON ORANGE SHERBET

Combine juice of 3 large lemons or 1 orange and 2 lemons, 1¼ c. sugar, ¼ tsp. salt. Stir in gradually 4 c. milk. The mixture will curdle; never mind. Freeze, stirring frequently.

ORANGE SHERBET

Combine and boil until it just barely spins a thread ½ c. each sugar and water. Dissolve 1 tsp. gelatin in 1 T. cold water, then add to sugar water. Cool. Add 1 c. orange juice, 1 T. lemon juice. Chill, then beat thoroughly and add ½ c. coffee cream. Freeze.

PINEAPPLE BUTTERMILK SHERBET

Mix thoroughly 1 qt. thick buttermilk, 1½ c. crushed pineapple, 1¼ c. sugar. Pour into freezing trays, freeze until mushy. Pour into chilled bowl and beat until smooth. Return to trays and continue freezing until firm. Yields 8–10 servings.

APRICOT BUTTERMILK SHERBET

Put 1 c. dried cooked apricots through a food mill or blender to make pulp. Add ½ c. sugar, 2 T. lemon juice, 1 T. brandy (optional). Stir until sugar is dissolved. Add 1 c. buttermilk. Pour into freezing trays and freeze as above. 4–6 servings.

THREE FRUIT SHERBET

Peel and mash 2 large bananas. Add juice of 3 oranges and 3 lemons, 2 c. sugar and 2 c. milk. When sugar is dissolved pour into freezing tray and freeze, stirring frequently. About 6 servings.

CRANBERRY SHERBET

Melt ¼ lb. marshmallows in ½ c. water or orange juice. Add 2 tsp. grated lemon rind, 1 lb. can cranberry sauce or jelly. Blend until smooth. Cool thoroughly. Fold chilled cranberry mixture into ½ c. whipped milk (method No. 1 page 80). Freeze as above.

BERRY SHERBET

Cover 1 qt. berries of choice with ½–1 c. sugar. Let stand 2 hrs.

Put through food mill or blender and then sieve. Add 1 T. lemon juice, 1 c. buttermilk. Mix, pour into freezing tray and freeze as above. 4–6 servings.

SWEET SAUCES AND ICINGS

BUTTERSCOTCH SAUCE (eggless and gluten free)

In saucepan mix   1 c. brown sugar, ¼ c. white sugar, ¼ tsp. salt
⅔ c. undiluted evaporated milk, ¼ c. butter or margarine, 2 T. corn syrup
Over medium heat, stirring, bring to boil and boil 3 min.
Cool slightly; add and mix 1 tsp. vanilla, ⅓ c. undiluted evaporated milk.

HOT FUDGE SAUCE
(eggless, milkless, and gluten free)

Melt in small pan   1 T. margarine or vegetable shortening
Add   2 squares unsweetened chocolate
Cook over low heat until chocolate is melted.
Add slowly, stirring ⅓ c. boiling water or coffee
Add and stir until dissolved 1 c. sugar, 2 T. white corn syrup
Simmer gently for 5 min.
Add ½ tsp. vanilla, dash of salt.
   Best used warm—good on ice cream, puddings, or plain cake.

LEMON SAUCE
(eggless, milkless, and gluten free)

In pan mix well   ½ c. sugar, 1 T. cornstarch
Slowly add   1 c. boiling water, dash of salt.
   Cook over low heat until mixture is smooth, thick and clear
Remove from heat and add 3 T. lemon juice, 1 tsp. grated lemon rind.

To make stronger lemon flavor substitute more lemon juice for part of water; to decrease lemon flavor reduce lemon juice, replace with water.

EASY CARAMEL SAUCE
(eggless and gluten free)

Melt over hot water 35–40 caramels (½ lb.)
Gradually stir in ¼ c. hot water, ⅛ tsp. salt
Blend thoroughly. Good hot or cold.

CARAMEL SAUCE NO. 2
(eggless, milkless, and gluten free)

In a heavy saucepan, over medium heat, stirring constantly, melt until it is liquid amber 3 T. white sugar. Do not burn it.
Remove from heat and slowly add 1 c. boiling water.
Stir until sugar is dissolved.
Mix together   1 scant c. sugar, 1½ T. cornstarch, ⅛ tsp. salt
Add slowly to make a paste ¼ c. cold water.
Stir into sugar water, cook about 5 min., stirring, until thick and clear.
Add   1 T. butter, margarine, or vegetable shortening,
          ½ tsp. vanilla.

FRUIT SAUCE
(eggless and gluten free)

Mix in pan   1½ c. fruit juice, ½ c. honey, ⅛ tsp. salt
          ⅛ c. margarine, 2 thin slices orange.
Bring to a boil, and boil 2–3 min.
Make a paste using 2 T. cornstarch, ½ c. juice.
Add slowly to boiling juice, cook until clear and thickened.

COCOA SAUCE
(eggless, milkless, and gluten free)

Combine   1 c. cocoa, 1¼ c. white sugar, ½ c. white corn syrup,
             1½ c. water, ⅛ tsp. salt.

Bring to a boil, cook slowly 5 min., stirring.
   Remove from heat and stir in 2 T. margarine or vegetable short-
      ening, 1 tsp. vanilla (optional).
Variation: Use part coffee for water, or add 1 tsp. instant coffee.

      Add rum flavoring instead of vanilla.

BITTERSWEET CHOCOLATE SAUCE
(eggless and gluten free)

Melt over low heat   2 squares unsweetened chocolate in 6 T.
                     water
Add   ½ c. sugar, ⅛ tsp. salt.
   Cook, stirring constantly, until sugar is dissolved and mixture
is slightly thickened.
Stir in   2 T. butter or margarine, ¼ tsp. vanilla.

HOT RUM SAUCE
(eggless and gluten free)

   Oh so good! Especially for holiday puddings.
Combine   ½ c. butter or margarine, 1 c. sugar, ½ c. water
Heat to boiling and boil 5 min.
Remove from heat; add ¼ c. rum, dash of cinnamon.
Serve hot.

HOT MINCEMEAT SAUCE
(eggless, milkless, and gluten free)

For plain puddings or ice cream

Combine   1½ c. bottled mincemeat, ⅓ c. undiluted frozen orange juice—thawed, ¼ c. water or 3 T. rum or brandy plus 1 T. water, 3 T. brown sugar.

Bring to a boil. Add ½ c. chopped nuts (optional).

FOAMY ORANGE SAUCE
(eggless and gluten free)

This will be quite firm when first made, and can be used this way if desired, but to have foamy foam sauce let it sit in refrigerator several hours after it is made.

Heat together to boiling point 1 c. orange juice, 2 T. lemon juice, ½ c. sugar

Make a thin paste of   1 T. cornstarch, 1 T. orange juice

Add cornstarch to hot juice, stirring constantly, and cook until thick and clear. Remove from fire.

Add   1 T. grated orange rind, dash of salt. Chill.

Prepare for whipping using method No. 2 under refrigerator desserts ½ c. evaporated milk. Whip and fold in chilled orange mixture. Refrigerate until ready to use.

Variations: Other fruit juices may be substituted for the orange.

BUTTER SAUCE
(eggless and gluten free)

Dissolve over medium heat 1 c. sugar, dash of salt in ½ c. half-and-half

Add   ½ c. soft margarine or butter, ½ tsp. vanilla

Mix well. Heat but do not boil. Serve hot over pudding or cake.

FROSTINGS AND ICINGS

These recipes have the texture of egg containing frostings but are eggless.

GLOSSY CHOCOLATE ICING
(eggless and gluten free)

Combine   2 c. sifted and packed powdered sugar, ¼ tsp. salt
Add   6 T. hot milk, 1 tsp. vanilla.
Stir until sugar is dissolved.
Melt over hot water 2 T. shortening, 1 T. butter, 2 oz. bitter
          chocolate.
   Add to sugar mixture and beat until smooth and thick enough
to spread.

CREOLE FROSTING
(eggless, milkless, and gluten free)

Pour   4 T. hot coffee over 2 c. packed powdered sugar
Stir until dissolved. Add ½ tsp. vanilla, ¼ tsp. salt
Melt over hot water   1 T. butter, 1 T. shortening (or 2 T.
                        shortening), 1 oz. bitter chocolate.
   Add to sugar mixture and beat until smooth and thick enough
to spread.

CARAMEL FROSTING (eggless and gluten free)

   Boil together 2 c. packed brown sugar and ⅔ c. evaporated
milk to soft ball stage (234°) and cool
Sift in   ⅔ c. packed powdered sugar.
   Beat until smooth and creamy. A little more milk may be
needed to keep frosting soft enough to spread easily.
   Chopped nuts may be mixed into the frosting or spread on
top while frosting is still soft.

CREAM CHEESE ICING AND FILLING
(eggless and gluten free)

   Mix thoroughly until well blended 1 (3 oz.) pkg. room temperature cream cheese, 2½ T. milk, 1½ c. sifted and packed powdered

sugar, ¼ tsp. salt, and ¾ tsp. vanilla. Spread on cake or between layers. Sprinkle with chopped nuts if desired.

PENOCHE FROSTING (eggless and gluten free)

Mix well in pan   1 lb. pkg. brown sugar, ⅔ c. milk, ⅔ c. shortening (part margarine) ¼ tsp. salt.

Bring rapidly to a boil, stirring constantly. Boil 1 min., or to 220° on candy thermometer. Remove from heat. Beat until cool enough and thick enough to spread. If it fails to thicken (it shouldn't) beat in a little more powdered sugar.

CREAMY ICING (eggless and gluten free)

Melt   ½ c. shortening—part margarine. Remove from heat.

Blend in   2½ T. flour (or 1 T. plus 1 tsp. cornstarch) ¼ tsp. salt

Stir in slowly   ½ c. milk.

Bring to a boil, stirring constantly. Boil 1 min. Remove from heat. Stir in about 3 c. sifted packed powdered sugar, ½ tsp. vanilla or flavoring of your choice. Beat to spreading consistency. (Place pan in ice water while beating to set more quickly.)

CREAMY BUTTER FROSTING (eggless and gluten free)

Cream until shiny   ¼ c. soft margarine or butter

Add slowly   2 c. sifted packed powdered sugar, ¼ tsp. salt 1 tsp. vanilla or ½ tsp. orange, lemon, or almond extract.

Gradually beat in   1–2 T. half-and-half or orange or lemon juice 1½ T. corn syrup.

(Use just enough corn syrup to produce a smooth spreading consistency.) Yield: enough for two 8-inch layers.

CRUNCHY CRUNCH TOPPING (eggless and gluten free)

Great for emergencies or those inevitable too busy days. Stores well in airtight container. Lovely on ice creams, mousses, sherbets, or plain puddings.

Melt in pan ¼ c. butter or margarine, ½ c. packed brown sugar

Cook over low heat, stirring constantly, to 250° or the hard ball stage. Remove from heat.

Add   1½ c. wheat or corn flakes, or gluten free cereal
                ⅓ c. chopped nuts (optional)

Stir until flakes are coated. Spread on cookie sheet to cool.

CREAMY FROSTING
(eggless, milkless, and gluten free)

Cream   6 T. soft vegetable shortening

Add   1 tsp. flavoring

Gradually add   1 pkg. sifted powdered sugar and enough hot water to give desired consistency. This is easiest made in an electric mixer.

2

Milkless Recipes Containing Egg

The most common offender in milk allergies is albumin; then perhaps the globulin. Cooking modifies these, often making them acceptable, as is demonstrated in the ability of many babies as well as other individuals to tolerate evaporated or cooked milk but not plain milk. The milk casein is less likely to cause problems; allergy tests and trial and error determine this.

A variety of milk substitutes are available on the market today. These must be approached with caution. Some of them are reconstituted dry milk. Some of the imitation milk products, such as Coffee Rich, and Cereal Blend contain casein as sodium caseinate, a salt, but no other milk ingredients. Where casein is not the offender, these products can replace milk. An imitation oleomargarine, 100 percent milk free, to use as a spread for breads, for vegetables, and meats is also available. Health food stores carry milk substitutes, 100 percent milk free, called Mocha Mix, a table cream substitute which can be diluted with water or fruit juice to reduce fat content, and dessert whip that will whip. The Mocha Mix, Cereal Blend, and Coffee Rich can be used in cooking. For soups, sauces, puddings, and pie fillings they replace milk readily. Puddings may need slightly more thickening to give the desired consistency. For baking cakes and cookies, shortening adjustment is necessary to compensate for the higher fat content of the milk substitutes.

In many recipes in which butter or margarine is specified, vegetable shortening and butter flavoring (this is optional and for flavoring purposes only) can be substituted. Exceptions are recipes where butter is important for texture, as in shortbreads. In meat, fish and vegetable cookery olive oil, bacon fat, peanut oil and sesame oil can be worthwhile substitutes for vegetable oils, margarine or butter. In many of the breads listed in Part I, potato or plain water, fruit or vegetable juice, with or without egg, can replace milk. (See Index for additional milkless recipes.)

BANANA ORANGE NUT BREAD (milkless)

Cream well	⅓ c. vegetable shortening
Gradually add	⅔ c. sugar. Cream until light and fluffy
Add	2 eggs (one at a time), beating well after each addition
To	2 T. concentrated (frozen) orange juice; add mashed banana to make 1 c.

Stir into above mixture. Add 1 tsp. orange rind.

Mix together	1¾ c. sifted flour, 2 tsp. baking powder, ¼ tsp. soda, ¾ tsp. salt.

Add in 3 or 4 portions. Mix until smooth after each. With last portion add ½ c. chopped nuts (optional). Spoon into well-greased loaf pan. Bake at 350° about 50 min. or until done. Cool on wire rack.

DEVIL'S FOOD CAKE (milkless)

This is easiest made in an electric mixer. Grease lightly two 8- or 9-inch cake pans. Cover bottoms with greased and floured waxed paper.

Sift together   1½ c. sifted flour, 1 c. sugar, ⅓ c. firmly packed brown sugar, ¾ tsp. salt, 1¼ tsp. soda, ¼ tsp. baking powder, ½ c. packed cocoa

Add   ½ c. soft vegetable shortening

Measure   ¾ c. water. Add 1 tsp. vanilla or rum flavoring, or 2–3 drops oil of peppermint.

Pour liquid into flour mixture. Beat at medium speed for 2 min. Add, one at a time, 2 large eggs. Beat 2 more min.

Add   ½ c. chopped nuts (optional).

Pour into prepared pans. Bake at 350° 30–40 min. When it tests done, remove to cake racks. Let stand 5 min. Invert and remove waxed paper from bottom. Finish cooling. Frost with brown sugar frosting.

BROWN SUGAR FROSTING (milkless)

This is a 7-minute type but easier and quicker.

Combine   1 egg white, 1 c. packed brown sugar, 3 T. water in top of double boiler. Stir until blended.

Place over rapidly boiling water. Beat until mixture is light and fluffy and will hold its shape. Easiest with an electric mixer.

ORANGE CAKE (milkless)

Cream   ⅓ c. shortening

Add slowly   1 c. sugar. Continue creaming until light and fluffy

Add, 1 at a time, 2 egg yolks, beating well after each addition.

Mix in   1–1½ T. grated orange peel.

Sift together   2 c. sifted cake flour, ½ tsp. soda, ¼ tsp. salt, ½ tsp. baking powder.

Beat until stiff 2 egg whites. Gradually beat in 1 T. sugar, set aside

Add   ¾ c. strained orange juice to creamed mixture alternately with the sifted flour.

Fold in egg whites.

Pour into greased 8 × 8 × 2-inch pan lined with greased waxed paper. Bake at 350° about 50 min. or until tests done with a toothpick. Cool on cake rack 5 min. Invert on second rack. Remove waxed paper to finish cooling. Serve with orange sauce, or cool and frost with orange confectioner's icing.

WHITE LAYER CAKE (milkless)

This is a very fine-textured and moist cake. Flavoring can be varied as desired. Best made in an electric mixer.

Cream	1 c. soft shortening until light
Slowly add	1 c. plus 2 T. sifted packed powdered sugar. Cream well
Add	1 tsp. vanilla
Sift together	4 times 2 c. sifted cake flour, 1 tsp. baking powder, ½ tsp. cream of tartar, ¼ tsp. salt
Measure	1 c. room temperature egg whites (about 8 large)
Add	¼ c. of egg whites to cream mixture. Beat hard.
	Repeat until ¾ of egg white is used.

Add remaining ¼ c. alternately with flour in 4–5 additions, beating until batter is smooth each time. Pour gently into two 8- or 9-inch pans which have been lightly greased and lined with greased waxed paper.

Bake about 30 min. at 325°. When done, remove to cake racks. Let stand 3–4 min. Invert gently. Remove waxed paper. Finish cooling. Frost as desired. It is especially good with fruit or lemon filling.

APRICOT UPSIDE DOWN CAKE (milkless)

An all-season cake, easy and good. Allow 4 hrs.

Add	½ c. boiling water to 1½ c. *moist* dried apricots.

Cover and let sit several hours. Drain off juice. There should be ¼ c. Add water if necessary.

Melt   ⅓ c. vegetable shortening, dash of salt, ⅔ c. packed brown sugar, ¼ c. white corn syrup in 8 × 8 × 2-inch pan.

Remove from heat. Place apricots cut side up onto the sugar mixture. Grease sides of pan.

Cream   ¼ c. soft shortening

Add   ½ c. sugar. Continue creaming until light and fluffy.

Add   ⅓ tsp. almond flavoring.

Beat in, one at a time, 2 eggs. Continue beating until light and smooth. Sift together 1 c. sifted cake flour, 1¼ tsp. baking powder, ¼ tsp. salt. Add alternately with the apricot juice in 2–3 portions, beating until smooth after each. Spoon batter gently over apricots, spreading gently. Bake at 350° about 35 min., or until cake tests done. Remove to cake rack. Let stand about 10 min. Invert onto serving plate. Serve warm or cold.

Variations: Substitute dried peaches, pears, apples, or prunes for apricots. Adjust flavoring as needed.

MILKLESS PUMPKIN DATE TORTE

This is a delicious dessert.

Mix together   ½ c. chopped dates, ½ c. chopped walnuts, 2 T. flour. Set aside.

Melt over low heat ¼ c. vegetable shortening. Add dash of salt

Add   1 c. firmly packed brown sugar. Blend in. Remove from heat.

Stir in   ⅔ c. canned pumpkin, 1 tsp. vanilla

Beat and add 2 eggs

Sift together   ½ c. sifted flour, ½ tsp. each baking powder, nutmeg, cinnamon, ¼ tsp. each ginger, and soda.

Add to pumpkin mixture. Mix thoroughly. Stir in floured dates and nuts. Pour into round 9 × 1½-inch cake pan—lightly greased and the bottom covered with greased and floured wax paper. Bake at 350° 20–25 min. Serve warm or cold, plain or with sauce of your choice.

ORANGE ICE BOX CAKE (milkless and gluten free)

Soften   1 T. plain gelatin in 1 T. cold water

Add   ¾ c. orange juice. Stand over hot water until gelatin dissolves.

Beat well   3 egg yolks. Gradually beat in ¾ c. sugar and orange juice.

Let cool, then fold in 1 tsp. grated orange rind, ½ tsp. grated lemon rind, 3 stiffly beaten egg whites.

Pour into 6-inch spring mold lined with macaroons (not the ones made with condensed milk). Chill 24 hrs. Remove mold and decorate with orange slices. Serves 6.

COFFEE ICE BOX CAKE
(eggless and gluten free)

Line a 6- or 7-inch mold with split lady fingers or gluten free cookies

Blend   ½ c. strong coffee with 1 T. cornstarch

Cook over hot water until slightly thickened

Pour on slowly   3 slightly beaten egg yolks. Return to double boiler. Cook until thick, about 3 min. Cool.

Cream   ⅓ c. vegetable shortening. For gluten free use butter

Beat in   ½ c. sifted and packed powdered sugar, ⅛ tsp. salt.

When smooth add the cold coffee mixture. Beat well.

Beat 3 egg whites until foamy. Gradually add ¾ c. packed powdered sugar. Beat until stiff and glossy. Gently fold into coffee mixture. Pour into cookie-lined mold. Chill 24 hrs.

CHOCOLATE ICE BOX CAKE
(eggless and gluten free)

Cream   ⅓ c. soft veg. shortening and dash of salt
              For gluten free use soft butter

Gradually add   ⅔ c. sifted and packed powdered sugar, 2 egg
          yolks
Beat very thoroughly.
Add   2 oz. melted bitter chocolate, ½ tsp. vanilla
Beat   2 egg whites until foamy. Gradually add ¾ c.
          packed powdered sugar
Beat until stiff and glossy. Gently fold in the chocolate mixture.

Line a 6-inch spring mold with split lady fingers or cookies as
above. Pour in chocolate mixture, chill 24 hrs. Remove mold rim.
Decorate with toasted cocoanut or nuts. Serves 6.

FRUIT CHIFFON PIE
(milkless and gluten free)

Prepare a 9-inch baked wheat or gluten free plain or crumb crust.
Measure   1¼ c. fruit juice of your choice—orange, pineapple,
berry, grape, apricot, prune etc., or use ¼–⅓ c. lemon juice
diluted with water to make 1½ c. Heat part of juice to dissolve
1 pkg. lemon gelatin. When completely dissolved stir in remaining
juice. Stir in ¾–1 c. sugar depending on sweetness of juice. Cool
until almost stiff.

Extra fruit or nuts (drained crushed pineapple, chopped apricots,
diced peaches, etc.) may be stirred in at this point.
Beat until stiff 3 egg whites. Continue beating, gradually adding
¼ c. sugar. Fold into gelatin mixture. Pile into crust. Chill until
serving time. Best used the day it is made.

3

Wheatless and Gluten-Free
Recipes

Living with wheatless diets is most difficult. Breadstuffs without gluten bear little similarity to breads as we normally accept them. Other cereals used in combination can approximate similar products but they may be very dense-textured, as in an all rye bread, or very crumbly, as in an all corn bread. The strong flavor of such cereal as buckwheat also presents problems, especially with children. Quick breads using more than one cereal give the best results.

The problem is even more complex with allergies, or with the nonabsorption syndrome when caused by gluten sensitivity which may be manifested as celiac disease in children and nontropical sprue in adults. In these latter cases the gluten acts as a poison in the intestinal tract, preventing absorption of not only gluten but many foods. The result can be starvation in the face of plenty. Not too long ago celiac children resembled children seen in pictures from lands where food is insufficient and starvation is in progress—large distended bellies and the rest of the body hardly more than skin and bones. Formerly these celiacs were kept alive on bananas; now with new understanding of the problem and proper care and treatment, these celiacs mature. Sprue can become a problem at any time of adult life.

In those cases where gluten must be eliminated, not only wheat but oats, rye, and barley as well as buckwheat must also be eliminated. This includes any product made with gluten-bearing ingredients such as malt and brewer's yeast made from barley mash, any cold cereal coated with malt, all commercial sauces, soups, puddings, baked products, alcoholic beverages from the offending grains, and all store-bought products which do not include a full list of ingredients. These problems are similar to those of egg-sensitive individuals who need to know the contents of all food products.

The elimination of gluten leaves rice, cornmeal, soybean and potato flours to work with. Removing gluten, which is composed of two proteins—gliaden and glutenin—removes the stretchy stickiness from doughs and batters which results when liquid is combined with gluten. Yeast can then no longer function as a leavener in breads since the yeast bubbles are no longer trapped in the little gluten balloons. A significant helper is eggs, which have a characteristic of expanding and holding, unlike gluten, but in a way that makes them almost indispensable for good gluten free cooking. They are also an asset because they tenderize and lighten texture.

Combining egg and other non-gluten products with the allowed basic flours makes the difference between heavy, soggy or crumbly, uninteresting food and food you can be proud to serve to anyone. These helpers are cornstarch, tapioca, and gelatin. In addition, combining very small amounts of potato flour gives an adhesiveness without sogginess.

Brown rice flour is the best all-around flour to replace wheat. A good basic starting point in developing your own recipes is 2 T. cornstarch in the bottom of a one-cup measuring cup and filled level with brown rice flour. A higher percentage of cornstarch is helpful for cakes and pastries as well as one to two tsp. of potato flour. More than normal amounts of baking powder are needed, and oftentimes less sugar than normally used results in better texture.

Brown rice flour can be found in some supermarkets; the other helpers are commonly found in all grocery stores. Soybean flour, rice polish, and rice bran, found in health-food stores, enrich the products nutritionally by giving more calcium, iron, thiamin, riboflavin, and niacin than whole wheat flour; and if a non-wheat diet is to be followed more than a short time, are well worth incorporating into the recipes. One half the rice flour can be replaced by either rice bran or rice polish, singly or in combination. Soya flour is heavy and can replace approximately one fourth of the total mixture.

Substituting for wheat in sauces, gravies, and puddings is not difficult. Cornstarch or tapioca replaces flour as a thickening agent for puddings and sweet sauces. Potato flour, rice flour, plain or combined with cornstarch, work well for gravies, soups, and unsweetened sauces.

Small-size baking pans give better results than large, and muffins and cookies are easier to make successfully than breads and cakes. Cookie recipes are the most adaptable and the easiest to convert from wheat recipes and therefore are given the least space here.

Included in this chapter are recipes for both plain wheat and gluten allergies and for gluten nonabsorption diets.

BANANA BREAD (gluten free)

Cream   5 T. shortening

Add gradually   ½ c. minus 1 T. sugar, 1 large egg.

Continue creaming until light and fluffy.

Into a 2 c. measure, put 1 T. potato flour, 1 T. minute tapioca, 1 T. cornstarch.

Fill c. to 1¾ level with unsifted brown rice flour.

Add   2½ tsp. baking powder, ½ tsp. salt, ½ tsp. soda.

Sift together 3 times. (The tapioca will not go through the sifter. Simply stir it into the sifted flour.)

Add dry ingredients to creamed mixture alternately with

1 c. mashed ripe bananas, ¼ c. buttermilk

Stir in (optional)   ½ c. chopped nuts, 1 tsp. grated orange rind.

Pour into 2 well greased 5 × 3 or 1 5 × 9-inch loaf pans. (Small containers give best results.) Bake at 350° 50–60 min. or until bread tests done when toothpick is inserted. Remove to cake rack, let stand 15–20 min. before removing from pan. Continue cooling. Store overnight before cutting.

This keeps well refrigerated or can be frozen.

PLAIN BREAD (gluten free)

This is a very good plain bread. It slices well and keeps well.

Stir   2 tsp. gelatin into ⅔ c. milk

Let stand 5 min. Warm enough to dissolve gelatin.

In bottom of measuring c. put 4 T. potato flour. Fill to ⅔ level with cornstarch

Sift together with   2½ c. rice flour, 2 T. baking powder, ¾ tsp. salt, 1 T. sugar

Put into mixing bowl. Make a well in flour.

Add   3 T. melted shortening or margarine
                      1 c. milk and gelatin milk, 2 well-beaten eggs.

Mix well and turn into 3 greased 5 × 3-inch or 1 9 × 5-inch loaf pans. Bake at 375° 15 min. Reduce temperature to 350° and continue baking about 30 min. for small loaves, 45–50 min. for the large loaf. Turn out onto wire rack. Cool thoroughly before cutting. This bread can be varied with soya, rice polish, or bran, but use them sparingly until you are familiar with the stronger flavor and slightly heavier texture. Start by substituting ¼ c. soya, polished rice or bran for ¼ c. brown rice flour. Chopped raisins or dates may also be added.

PUMPKIN BREAD (gluten and milk free)

This is a fine-textured delicious sweet bread. It keeps well.

Stir into   1 c. pumpkin 1 T. minute tapioca, 2 large eggs.

Set aside 15 min. or until tapioca softens.

Into a 1 c. measure put 2 T. potato flour, 3 T. cornstarch.

Fill to 1 c. level with brown rice flour.

Add an additional   ¾ c. rice flour, 1 T. baking powder, ¾ tsp. soda, 1 tsp. cinnamon, ½ tsp. salt, ½ tsp. nutmeg or coriander.

Sift all together three times.

Cream   ⅓ c. vegetable shortening

Adding 1–2 T. at a time and beating after each addition until sugar is thoroughly blended, add 1 c. packed, lump-free brown sugar

Add pumpkin-egg mixture. Beat well.

Stir flour into creamed mixture in 3–4 additions, ½–¾ c. chopped nuts may be added with last addition of flour. Pour into a well-greased 9 × 5 × 3-inch pan or three 5 × 3-inch pans. Bake at 350° 40–45 min. for small loaves or 60–65 min. for large loaf. Let cool 15–20 min. in pans on rack. Remove from pans, continue cooling. Let stand several hours or overnight before cutting.

SOUR CREAM BREAD (gluten free)

Measure   2 tsp. gelatin into ⅓ c. milk. Let stand 5 min. Heat just enough to dissolve gelatin and melt 3 T. margarine

Add   ⅓ c. cold milk

Stir milk into 2 slightly beaten large eggs

Stir in   ⅓ c. sugar (brown or white), 1 c. commercial sour cream

In a 1 c. measure put 4 T. potato flour. Fill to ⅔ c. level with cornstarch.

Sift together 3 times with: 2 c. plus 6 T. brown rice flour, 2 T. baking powder, ¾ tsp. salt.

Stir into liquid mixture and blend well. Mixture should almost hold its shape. Spoon into 3 well-greased 5 × 3-inch tins. Bake at 375° 15 min. Reduce temperature to 350°. Continue baking another 30 min. or until done. It should be golden brown.

Turn out onto rack to cool.

Variations: Add 1 c. raisins, chopped dates, nuts, or ½ tsp. cinnamon.

OATMEAL AND RYE BREAD
(wheat and egg free)

Pour   3 c. buttermilk over 2 c. quick cooking oats

Let stand 10–15 min. Add ⅔ c. packed brown sugar

Sift together 2¼ c. sifted rye flour, 1 tsp. salt, 2 tsp. soda, 1 tsp. baking powder. Mix well into oatmeal buttermilk mixture.

Spoon into well greased 9 × 5-inch loaf pan. Bake at 325° 30 min. Reduce temperature to 300°. Continue baking about 1 hr. or until bread tests done with a toothpick. Cool on wire rack about 5 min., turn out onto wire rack. Let cool before slicing.

SOUR CREAM CORNBREAD
(gluten free)

Light and tender, easy to make, good to eat. Bake in a heavy 9- or 10-inch skillet or frying pan which has been preheated in a 450° oven about 10 min. before pan is filled with batter.

Measure and set aside 3 T. shortening (if regular sour cream is used; 4 T. if half-and-half sour cream is used).

Combine   1 c. sifted cornmeal, ⅓ c. cornstarch, 2 tsp. baking powder, ¼ tsp. soda, 1 tsp. salt, 2 T. sugar. Resift twice.

To   1 c. sour cream add 2 egg yolks. Beat until creamy.
Remove skillet from oven. Put in shortening to melt.
Add sour cream mix to dry ingredients. Beat until well mixed.
Add melted shortening from hot skillet.

Beat until stiff but not dry 1 egg white. Fold into above mixture.
Pour into hot skillet immediately. Bake at 450° about 30 min.
Serve piping hot. Yield: 6–8 wedges.

CORNMEAL BREAD
(gluten free and eggless)

Stir   1 envelope gelatin into ½ c. buttermilk. Let sit
              5 min.
Warm enough to dissolve gelatin. Cool.
Pour   1½ c. buttermilk over 1 c. cornmeal, 2 T. potato
              buds
Let sit while measuring flour.
Sift together 1 c. plus 2 T. rice flour, 1 tsp. salt, 2 tsp. soda,
              1 tsp. baking powder
To cornmeal buttermilk mix add gelatin buttermilk, ¼ c. molasses,
              2 T. brown sugar. Blend.
Stir in flour.

Pour into three 3 × 5-inch or one 3½ × 7½-inch, or one 5 ×
9-inch pans which have been greased and sprinkled with cornmeal. Bake at 300° 50 min. for the small loaves, 60–65 min.
for the large.
Turn out onto wire rack to cool.

BISCUITS MUFFINS
(gluten free)

This recipe makes a light and tender muffin or drop biscuit
which holds its shape very well. The dough is too soft to roll but
can be dropped into a lightly greased pan for biscuits or into
greased muffin tins. The method is as for biscuits.

In a 1 c. measure, put 3 T. cornstarch. Fill with brown rice flour.

Add   1 T. potato flour, 2 tsp. baking powder, ¼ tsp. soda, ¼ tsp. salt

Cut in   3 T. firm butter or margarine

Beat   1 large egg. Add ½ c. buttermilk

Stir into dry ingredients to make a muffin-consistency dough.
Bake at 425° 12–15 min. or until golden brown.

PANCAKES (gluten free)

Delicious!

In measuring c. put 4 T. cornstarch. Fill to 1 c. level with brown rice flour.

Sift three times with 2 tsp. baking powder, 4 tsp. sugar, ⅛ tsp. salt
Put into mixing bowl.

Beat lightly together 2½ T. oil, ¾ c. milk, 2 large eggs

Add all at once to dry ingredients. Stir until mixed. Bake on hot greased griddle, or at 400° if thermostatically controlled. Milk can be increased or decreased to give thicker or thinner batter.

Variations: ¼ c. rice bran or polish, or soya flour can replace the same amount of flour. Yield: 8–10 pancakes.

CORNMEAL POTATO PANCAKES
(gluten free)

Sift together 3 times   ¼ c. cornmeal, ¼ c. brown rice flour 4 tsp. cornstarch, 2 tsp. baking powder, 1 tsp. soda, ¼ tsp. salt 4–5 tsp. sugar. Put into mixing bowl.

In a smaller bowl put   ¼ c. lumpless mashed potatoes, 2 large lightly beaten eggs, 2½ T. oil, ¾ c. buttermilk.

Stir into flour mixture and proceed as above.

OATMEAL AND RYE PANCAKES
(wheatless)

Thin and tender with a pleasant flavor.

Mix together   1½ c. quick oats, 2 c. buttermilk. Let stand 5 min.

Sift together   ½ c. sifted rye flour, 1 tsp. each sugar, soda, salt

Add to buttermilk and oats. Stir until well mixed.

Add   2 well beaten eggs.

Cook as above. Yield: about 1 doz.

SWEDISH FLATBREAD
(gluten free and eggless)

In a 1 c. measure put 2 T. potato flour. Fill c. level with corn-starch. Sift together three times with 2 c. rice flour, 3½ T. sugar, 1 tsp. soda, 1 tsp. salt

Proceed as for Flatbread (page 40).

These make an excellent cracker for gluten free diets. The sugar can be decreased if desired.

OATMEAL AND RYE MUFFINS
(wheat free)

Scald   1 c. milk.

Stir in   1 c. quick cooking oats, 2 T. margarine or shorten-
             ing, 1 tsp. salt, ⅓ c. brown sugar. Cool.

Add   1 scant c. milk, 3 well-beaten egg yolks

Sift together 1 c. sifted rye flour, 4 tsp. baking powder

Add to oat mixture. Spoon quickly into greased muffin tins.

Bake at 425 ° 18–20 min. Yield: 8–10 muffins.

OATMEAL AND WHITE CORNMEAL MUFFINS
(wheat free)

In preceding recipe substitute 1⅓ c. white cornmeal, 2 T. cornstarch, for rye flour.

COOKIES

Cookies are the least difficult gluten free recipes. Many wheat recipes adapt very easily. Therefore only a few sample recipes are included here.

BASIC COOKIES (gluten free)

Rich and crispy, adaptable to many variations. It keeps well in an air tight container or frozen.

Sift together 3 times	½ c. cornstarch, 2 tsp. potato flour, 1½ c. brown rice flour, ¼ tsp. salt, ½ tsp. baking powder, ½ tsp. soda
Cut in	1 c. margarine or part butter
Beat	2 large eggs until thick and lemon-colored
Add	¼ c. buttermilk, 1 tsp. vanilla, ½ tsp. rum or other flavoring. Stir gently into flour mixture.

Use two spoons to shape cookies. They will be quite sticky to handle. Place on greased baking sheet. They may be gently flattened with a rice-floured glass to smooth the top. Bake on middle rack of oven at 325° about 30 min. They will be less rich if ¾ c. shortening is used.

Variations: Add chocolate chips, chopped nuts, dates, or raisins or candied fruit.

Chocolate Cookies: Replace 2 T. rice flour with 2 T. cocoa. Roll unbaked cookies in cinnamon and sugar, or cocoa and sugar.

Add	nutmeg, cinnamon, or other spices to the flour
Add	almond, orange or lemon flavoring and grated rind to replace vanilla and rum flavoring.

SPECIAL COOKIES (gluten free)

In measuring c. put 2 tsp. potato flour, 2 tsp. cornstarch.

Fill to 1 c. level with brown rice flour. Place in mixing bowl.

Add   2 T. sugar, brown or white

Cut in   ⅓ c. butter as for pie crust

Part 1

Pat very thinly into 9 × 16-inch greased pan. Bake at 350° about 20 min. on middle shelf of oven until golden brown. Watch it carefully.

Part 2

Mix together   1½ c. brown sugar, 1 c. chopped nuts, ⅓–½ c. shredded cocoanut.

Sift together three times 1 T. potato flour, 4 tsp. cornstarch, 3 T. brown rice flour, 1 tsp. baking powder, ⅛ tsp. salt.

Add to brown sugar mixture. Mix thoroughly.

Beat until light and *thick* 2 large eggs. Add 1 tsp. vanilla.

Stir into above mixture. Spread this over the baked crust.

Bake again at 300° about 30 min. or until toothpick comes out clean.

Partially cool. Cut into squares. Served with a spoon of whipped cream, this is a complete dessert.

BROWNIES (gluten and milk free)

These are delicious and keep well several days—if they have a chance.

Melt together over hot water 2 sq. unsweetened chocolate (2 oz.)
                           ⅓ c. shortening (part butter if allowed).

Cool slightly. Transfer to mixing bowl.

Beat in gradually   ½ c. minus 1 T. brown sugar, ½ c. minus 1 T. white sugar, 2 eggs, slightly beaten.

The mixture should be quite stiff.

Measure and sift well   ½ c. unsifted brown rice flour, 2 T. cornstarch, 1 tsp. baking powder, ½ tsp. salt

Stir into chocolate mixture. Add ½ c. chopped nuts.

Pour into well greased 8 × 8 × 2-inch pan. Bake at 350° 30–35 min. A dull crust will appear on top of brownies as they bake. Test with a toothpick.

Cool on rack in pan. Cut into squares.

CAKES

Gluten free cakes can be amazingly good as long as a generous amount of egg can be used.

BANANA CAKE (gluten free)

Delicious!

Measure   1¼ c. rice flour, ½ c. cornstarch, 1½ tsp. baking powder, 1½ tsp. soda, ¾ tsp. salt

Sift together 3 times, set aside.

In mixing bowl cream   ½ c. soft shortening

Gradually add   1 c. plus 2 T. sugar

Add, one at a time, beating well after each, 4 large eggs.

Stir in   1 c. mashed ripe bananas (3–4 bananas)

Add flour alternately with   ½ c. buttermilk.

Pour into two 8-inch cake pans, greased and lined with greased waxed paper. Bake at 350° for about 40 min. Loosen edges, invert on wire rack, remove paper and continue cooling.

CHOCOLATE CAKE (gluten free)

This feathery-light cake is delicious!

Cream   ½ c. soft shortening

Add gradually   1¼ c. sugar and continue creaming

Add   4 large eggs, one at a time. Beat well after each addition

Stir in   6 T. cocoa mixed with 5 T. water

Add ½ c. buttermilk alternately with dry ingredients.

Stir well together 2 T. cornstarch, 2 tsp. potato flour

Fill c. to   1⅓ c. level with brown rice flour.

Add   1 tsp. salt, 1½ tsp. soda, 1 tsp. baking powder. Sift three times.

Have ready two 8-inch cake pans, greased and lined with waxed paper and dusted with cocoa. Divide batter between pans. Bake at 350° 30–35 min. or until cake tests done. Remove from oven, invert on wire rack, remove paper and cool. Frost as desired.

GOLDEN CAKE (gluten free)

Cream   ½ c. soft shortening

Add gradually 1 c. plus 2 T. sugar, continue creaming

Add   4 large eggs, one at a time, beating well after each addition

Stir in   2 T. grated orange rind, ½ tsp. orange extract

Sift all together three times 6 T. cornstarch, 2 tsp. potato flour.

Fill c. to 1 c. level with rice flour. Add ¾ c. more, 2 tsp. baking powder, 1 tsp. cream of tartar, ½ tsp. salt.

Add alternately with ¾ c. milk.

Prepare two 8-inch layer pans as above dusting pans with powdered sugar. Bake at 350° 30–35 min. Cool as above.

CHIFFON CAKE (gluten free and milkless)

Put   2 T. cornstarch in measure

Fill to ½ c. with brown rice flour.

Sift together 3 times with 1 tsp. potato flour, ⅓ c. plus 1 T. sugar, 1 tsp. baking powder, ½ tsp. cream of tartar, ¼ tsp. salt.

Put into mixing bowl.

Make a well. Add in order 2 T. oil, 3 egg yolks, 1½ T. water, 1 tsp. vanilla, 1 tsp. grated lemon rind.

Beat with a spoon until smooth.

Beat until frothy   ¼ c. egg whites (room temperature)

Add   ¼ tsp. cream of tartar.

Continue beating until whites form very stiff peaks.

Fold very gently into yolk mixture. Spoon gently into foil-lined 9 × 5 × 3-inch pan. Do not grease. Bake at 325° 30–35 min. or until cake tests done. Invert to cool.

Variations: Orange juice and rind can replace the water, vanilla, and lemon rind. Almond extract (½ tsp.) can replace the vanilla and rind. Spices can be added.

MISCELLANEOUS GLUTEN FREE DESSERTS

These recipes give good nutritional variety to gluten free diets.

BAKED APPLE PUDDING
(gluten free)

Heat   1 c. milk

Pour over   1½ c. gluten free bread or muffin crumbs mixed with ¼ tsp. salt, ½ tsp. ginger, ¼ tsp. mace, ¼ tsp. cloves

Add   ½ c. raisins, 1½ c. peeled chopped apples, ½ c. chopped nuts (optional), 3 T. fruit juice or brandy

Beat   2 small or 1½ large eggs

Beat in gradually   ½ c. sugar until thick and lemon-colored

Add   1 tsp. baking powder.

Stir into bread mixture. Pour into well greased casserole. Bake at 350° about 1 hr. Serve plain, with fruit or custard sauce. Best served warm.

LEMON SPONGE (gluten free)

This is a wheatless version of an old-time favorite. It is as delicious as the original.

Sift together   1 c. sugar, ¼ tsp. salt, 2 T. cornstarch, 2 T. brown rice flour

Add   ¼ c. lemon juice, 2 egg yolks, lightly beaten

With a whip, egg beater, or big spoon beat mixture well.

Add and stir in   ½–¾ tsp. grated lemon rind, 1½ T. melted butter or margarine, 1 c. milk.

Beat until stiff 2 egg whites.

Fold into above mixture until well blended. Pour into buttered casserole 7–8-inches by 3 inches deep, or into individual molds. Set in pan of hot water. Bake at 325° 40–50 min. or until inserted knife comes out clean. Remove to rack to cool. Best served lukewarm or cold. 6 servings.

Variations: Orange Sponge. Replace lemon rind and juice with 1 tsp. grated orange rind, ¼ c. strained orange juice with 1 T. lemon juice.

Lime Sponge. Substitute ¼ c. lime juice for the lemon juice.

BRANDY PUFF
(gluten free and milkless)

An easy and appealing dessert. Company or family fare.

Combine in pan   ½ c. pkd. brown sugar, ½ c. chopped walnuts, ½ c. light seedless raisins, 1 c. thick applesauce, 1 tsp. cinnamon, ¼ tsp. nutmeg, ⅛ tsp. ginger, ¼ c. apricot brandy.

Bring to a boil, stirring occasionally.

Beat   2 room temperature egg whites until stiff peaks form

Gradually add   ¼ c. sugar. Beat until very stiff.

Pile on top of cooked mixture in a baking dish. Bake at 325° 15–20 min. or until meringue is a delicate brown. Serve at once. Serves 4. Recipe may be doubled. Other brandy flavors or apricot juice may be substituted.

NORWEGIAN PRUNE PUDDING
(gluten free and milkless)

Wash ½ lb. prunes (about 22). Soak in 2 c. cold water. Remove pits and return prunes to same water.

Add   1 c. sugar, 1 inch piece of stick cinnamon or 1 tsp. ground cinnamon, 1⅓ c. boiling water

Simmer for 10 min.

Gradually add   ⅓ c. orange juice or water to ⅓ c. cornstarch

Add to prune mixture. Cook 5 min., stirring gently until thickens and cornstarch is cooked. Remove stick cinnamon. Add 1 T. lemon juice. Pour into serving dishes. About 8 servings.

BAKED PRUNE WHIP
(gluten free and milkless)

Prepare prunes by simmering gently in water (2 c. fruit to 1½ c. water) until tender with ½ c. sugar (optional).

Pit and chop very fine enough prunes to make 1 c.

Add   2 tsp. grated orange rind, 2 T. orange juice, 1 tsp. grated lemon rind

Chop   ½ c. nuts

Add   Dash of salt to 4 room temperature egg whites

Beat until they hold stiff peaks. Gradually add ⅓ c. sugar. Continue beating until shiny and will hold stiff peaks. Remove and clean off beaters. Gently fold in prune puree. Fold in nuts with last of puree.

Spoon gently into a 6 c. casserole. Set in pan of water 1 inch deep. Bake at 350° about 35 min. or until wisps of brown appear on top of whip.

Cool slightly (out of a draft) before serving. Serve plain or with orange or lemon sauce.

Variations: Substitute other dried fruits for the prunes. Adjust sugar as needed.

PUMPKIN DATE TORTE
(gluten free and milkless)

See milkless pumpkin date torte. Substitute as follows:

Use 2 T. rice flour for wheat flour on chopped dates and nuts. Substitute ½ c. sifted rice flour for wheat flour and use 1 tsp. baking powder. Proceed according to directions.

DEVIL'S FOOD CAKE
(gluten free and milkless)

Follow recipe for milkless devils food (page 97), making the following changes:

Use 1 c. sifted brown rice flour, ½ c. cornstarch, ½ tsp. baking powder

Use 3 large eggs.

ORANGE MARMALADE STEAMED PUDDING
(gluten free)

This is excellent made with pumpkin bread but other gluten free breads can be used.

Pour	1 c. milk over 3 c. fine soft bread crumbs
Add	½ c. melted shortening, 1 slightly beaten egg
Blend in	½ c. orange marmalade, 2 T. brown sugar for sweet bread, ¼ c. for plain, ½ tsp. brandy or rum flavoring

Sift together and add   1 c. sifted brown rice flour, 1½ tsp. soda, 1 tsp. salt, 1 tsp. baking powder.

For plain bread add 2½ tsp. pumpkin pie spice mix or 1 tsp. cinnamon, ¾ tsp. nutmeg, ½ tsp. ginger.

For spiced breads, add spices as desired.

Add   1 c. chopped dates or chips; or ½ c. each chopped dates and nuts.

Mix well.

Steam in greased 1½-qt. mold or its equivalent for 3 hrs.

Serve hot with fruit or vanilla sauce, or flame brandy with sugar lumps soaked in orange or lemon extract.

CHEESE SOUFFLÉ (gluten free)

As good as any you have eaten!

Make a thick white sauce using 1 T. rice flour, 1 T. potato flour, 1 T. cornstarch, well mixed, 4 T. butter, 1 c. milk

Add   ¼ tsp. A-1 sauce, ¼ tsp. mustard

Add   1 c. shredded sharp cheddar cheese

Separate   3 large eggs.

Beat yolks well and stir gently into white sauce. This is easiest if you spoon a little sauce into the yolks and mix well before putting into larger amount.

Beat whites until foamy. Add ½ tsp. cream of tartar.

Continue beating until stiff but not dry.

Fold yolk mixture gently into whites. Pile into ungreased 1½-qt. casserole. Set casserole in pan of water in middle of oven. Bake at 350° about 60 min. Serve immediately.

PIE CRUST (gluten free)

This amount makes two 9-inch shells or one double crust. It

is very tender. It cannot be picked up, like regular flour crust, without breaking. It is easiest to roll it on a well-floured pastry cloth using a pastry stocking on the rolling pin.

To place in the pan, lift pastry cloth from one end, flip the crust over the pie plate. Gently ease into position. If the edges break they can be pressed together.

In a 2 c. measure put 4 T. cornstarch.

Fill level with brown rice flour.

Add   1 tsp. salt, 4 tsp. baking powder

Sift well together.

Cut in   1 scant c. shortening.

Beat well   1 large egg and stir in (no other liquid is used).

Pat into a ball. Divide in two. Roll gently. Place in pan. Sprinkle crust with sugar. Chill in refrigerator before baking.

Bake at 425° about 10 min., or until delicately browned.

Part II
Fish and Meats

4
Egg, Milk, Wheat, and Gluten-Free Recipes

The following fish and meat recipes are excellent examples of what can be accomplished in the best of eating and still stay within the confines of food limitations.

Where dips and binders for meats and fish become a problem, substitutions can be made. Eggs are generally used in loaves, patties, or rolls with stuffing. When eggs must be eliminated, canned milk, half-and-half, or undiluted cream soup normally will do. A little gelatin or minute tapioca can be added for firmer texture. For stuffing or filling use bread that is not completely dry, or moisten crumbs in a little milk, water, or broth in which a little minute tapioca has softened 10–15 min.

To replace an egg dip as an adhesive for crumbs try dipping in either milk or melted margarine, which gives a crisper-textured coating. It is excellent for broiling lean fish or for pan-frying. Try experimenting also with tomato juice or diluted lemon juice where the flavor is compatible.

Meat, fish, and salad mousses can be made using whipped unsweetened evaporated milk (see method No. 2 page 80) using ⅓ c. dry skim milk and 2 T. lemon juice (no sugar) for each ½ c. evaporated milk.

The following wheatless recipes are also gluten free.

FISH

The delicate flavor of much fish is lost in the cooking. With fish that is fried in heavy batters and those with heavy sauces and embellishments the flavor of the adornments predominate. If you like fish and have not tried poaching as well as broiling and baking please do.

POACHED FILET OF SOLE OR OTHER FILETED WHITE FISH
(eggless, milkless, and wheatless)

Boned filets are more appealing than unboned slices, but either can be used. Use an electric frypan or skillet with a tight lid. Cover bottom with foil. Lay filets so they do not overlap. Make cooking sauce (recipe under fish sauces). Pour over filets and cover tightly. Simmer just until fish is done. Pat on a little butter (optional). Sprinkle with paprika and parsley. The juice can be slightly thickened or spooned as is onto the fish.

BROILED FISH (eggless, milkless, and wheatless)

Simplicity is again the essential element for success. Place fish in baking pan lightly greased. Broil about 4 inches from heat. Baste frequently with cooking sauce (see above). When one side is done turn carefully and repeat broiling and basting. Very thin filets do not require turning. The thickness of the fish determines the cooking time. Just before it is done salt fish lightly, spread lightly with butter or substitute, and serve with remaining sauce which should have thickened some during the cooking.

BAKED FISH (eggless, milkless, and wheatless)

Larger pieces of fish may be baked and basted with the same sauce.

PIQUANT WHITE FISH FILETS
(eggless, milkless, and wheatless)

Use the white fish of your choice, Red snapper, halibut, turbot, or sole are all excellent. Others are equally good.

Two lbs. of fillets will make 4–6 servings. Cut fish into serving-size pieces. Salt and sprinkle with chopped parsley. Don't be stingy. Allow to stand 20 min.

To make sauce, cream together   ¼ c. butter or substitute (see page 97)
                                  2 T. flour or substitute (see page 104)
                                  ½ tsp. dry mustard
                                  ½ tsp. onion powder*
Add and mix well   1 tsp. soy sauce
                                  2 T. lemon juice
                                  ½ c. warm water

Use baking dish with a tight cover. Cover bottom of dish with not more than half the sauce. Arrange fish on sauce.

Cover with   1½ c. sliced fresh mushrooms
               1 T. capers

Pour remaining sauce gently over all. Cover. Bake at 350° until fish flakes easily when tested with a fork—15–25 min. depending on thickness of fish.

BROILED FISH FILETS A LA GREECE
(eggless, milkless, and wheat free)

Filet of sole is excellent but any mild-flavored non-oily fish

---

* 2 T. minced onions combined with capers may be substituted for onion powder

128 Creative Cooking without Wheat, Milk and Eggs

fillet may be substituted. Frozen fish may also be used, if thawed so fillets can be separated; 2 lbs. will make 6 servings. Pat fish dry. Place in bowl or pan. Make a marinade of ⅓ c. olive oil, ⅓ c. lemon juice, 2 tsp. finely chopped mint leaves or 1 tsp. dried mint, ½ tsp. salt, pepper to taste. Spoon marinade over fish to cover. Let sit about 15 min. Place on broiler pan. Broil just until tender. Pour juice over fish when serving.

ROLLED FILET OF SOLE
(eggless, milkless, and wheatless)

For 6 servings use 1½–1¾ lbs. filets. Pieces may need to be pieced together by lapping edges to give similar sized servings.

Chop very fine and combine	2 stalks of celery
	1 medium-sized onion
	½ c. blanched almonds (optional)
	1 clove garlic crushed (or ¼ tsp. garlic powder)
Sauté about 5 min. in	2 T. butter, margarine, or vegetable shortening
Add	¼ c. canned chicken broth
	1 c. soft bread crumbs or wheat substitute
Season with	1 tsp. salt
	pinch of nutmeg or allspice
	pinch of mace

Divide equally onto filets. Roll up and fasten with toothpicks. Melt ¼ c. butter or margarine, or use olive or salad oil for milk—less to cover bottom of baking dish. Arrange fish rolls on top. Sprinkle rolls with 2 T. lemon juice or ¼ c. white wine.
Bake at 450° for 5 min. Turn carefully and bake another 5 min. or just until fish is cooked through.

Serve with lemon wedges or dill or shrimp sauce.

OVEN-FRIED WHITE FISH
(eggless, milkless, and wheatless)

Mix together equal quantities of lemon juice and melted butter, margarine or olive oil. Dip pieces of fish into this and then into fine dry bread crumbs or cornmeal. Place on broiler and broil about 4 inches from heat until fish is nicely browned. Turn carefully and repeat on other side until brown and tender. Serve with lemon wedges or sauce.

BAKED RED SNAPPER WITH SAVORY TOMATO SAUCE
(eggless, milkless, and wheatless)

Dredge 2½–3 lbs. red snapper filets lightly in flour or substitute. Place in lightly greased baking pan. Salt fish. Cover with tomato sauce (recipe below), sprinkle with parsley and bake at 350° about 40–45 min. Other fish may be substituted.

Sauce: In a medium sized sauce pan put:

> 2 cans stewed tomatoes
> 1½ tsp. Worcestershire sauce
> ½ lemon finely sliced
> 1 bay leaf
> ½ tsp. basil

Heat to boiling. Remove from fire, cover and let steep 10–15 min. Put through food mill, strainer, or into blender and then strain. This amount can be cut in half for smaller amounts or for tomato shrimp sauce. (See shrimp sauces No. 1, p. 137) This recipe makes 6–8 generous servings.

BAKED FINNAN HADDIE
(eggless and gluten free)

Boil 2 lbs. finnan haddie until tender.

Boil 24 small onions and 1 sliced green pepper.

Arrange fish and onions in baking dish.

Make a white sauce of   1½ T. butter

> 2 T. flour or substitute (see p. 104)
> 1 tsp. salt

Add   1 (13 oz.) can of milk.

Stir until smooth and thickened. Pour over fish.

Top with 1 c. bread crumbs or substitute lightly browned in

4 tsp. butter. Sprinkle with parsley. Bake at 350° 15–20 min. or until bubbly and heated through. Serves 6–8.

MIXED SEAFOOD EN BROCHETTE WITH DILL SAUCE
(wheat, milk, and egg free)

Any desired combination of shrimp, crab, scallops, lobster, and oysters may be used. Also needed are mushrooms, butter or substitute, and lemon. Individual fish pieces may be skewered on toothpicks as hors d'oeuvres with the sauce served as a dip. A small skewerful served with crisp toast or crackers is also good as a first course. Two 6-inch skewers make a wonderful entree.

For a combination of prawns, scallops, and oysters for 12 skewers use about 1½ lbs. each of prawns and scallops and 1 pt. small fresh or canned oysters.

For court bouillon to cook prawns combine 1½ qts. water, ½ lemon sliced, 1 large piece celery with leaves, 1 bay leaf, 3–4 peppercorns, ½ onion sliced, 1 small clove garlic, ¾ tsp. salt, ¼ tsp. sugar, pepper to taste. Bring to boil and simmer covered 15–20 min. Add prawns. They should be well covered. Simmer gently 5–6 min. or until they turn a delicate pink. Overcooking toughens them. Remove prawns from court bouillon. Add a few of the shells to it as you de-shell the prawns. Boil the bouillon down to approximately 3 c. Set aside for the Dill Sauce.

Wrap oysters in ½ slice bacon. If oysters are not used, crab or scallops may be wrapped; or bacon pieces about 1 inch square may be placed loosely between the pieces of fish on the skewer. Do not crowd. The skewers can be filled well ahead of serving time, placed on wax paper, and refrigerated until 15 min. before serving time. The Dill Sauce can also be made in advance and reheated to serve.

Remove skewers from refrigerator 20 min. before cooking time. Place well apart on broiler.

Melt ¾ c. butter, margarine, or use salad oil for milkless. Add ¼ c. lemon juice. Whip until well mixed. Brush well onto fish. Place about 3 inches under broiler. Broil approximately 5 min. Turn skewers. Brush with more lemon butter, add a medium-sized buttered mushroom to end of skewer and broil 5 min. more. Serve hot with hot Dill Sauce (recipe under fish sauces).

BROILED PRAWNS (egg, wheat, and milk free)

Frozen prawns prepared according to directions under mixed seafood en brochette, or large shrimp may be used. These may be completely prepared for cooking in advance and refrigerated until time to broil. They are lovely served as hors d'oeuvres with just a toothpick inserted in each, or served as an entrée on toast or rice—plain or with dill or lemon mustard sauce. Allow 5–6 prawns per serving or more depending on size. For 30 prawns— cleaned and dry—combine in a small bowl 2 T. lemon juice, 2 T. water, 3 T. olive or salad oil. Dip prawns, one at a time, into above, then into a mixture of ½ c. fine dry bread crumbs (using either wheat or wheat free bread), ½ tsp. powdered ginger, 1 tsp. garlic salt, 1 tsp. finely chopped parsley.

Be sure prawns are completely coated with crumbs. Place well apart on foil-covered cookie sheet ready for broiling. If they are to be refrigerated, return to room temperature 20 min. before broiling time. Broil 3–4 inches from heat for 2–3 min. or until gently browned. Turn carefully and repeat. Serve immediately.

SHRIMP SUPREME (wheat, milk, and egg free)

This is a wonderful blending of flavors. It can be prepared ahead of time and refrigerated until 20 min. before cooking time.

Melt   ¼ c. butter, margarine, or vegetable shortening and butter flavoring

Add   2 T. minced shallots, green onions, or ½ tsp. onion powder, 1 clove garlic finely minced, or ¼ tsp. garlic powder, ½ tsp. *each* chervil leaves, ground nutmeg, parsley, tarragon leaves, salt, mei-yen or aji-no-moto (Accent)—mei-yen is a seasoning salt put out by Spice Island. Aji-no-moto is the same as Accent. It is the oriental term but is found in many markets. ¼ tsp. thyme 1 c. dry bread crumbs—wheat or substitute (See page 106)

Mix well.

Add   ½ c. dry sherry or chicken stock with lemon juice.

In individual casseroles or shells alternate this mixture with ¾ lb. cooked, cleaned, dry shrimp—fresh or canned—ending with a layer of crumbs.

Bake at 400° for 20 min. Serve immediately. Serves 6.

SHRIMP STUFFED EGGPLANT
(wheat, milk, and egg free)

This combines fish and vegetable into an interesting entrée.

Cut a 2 lb. eggplant in half lengthwise. Scoop out the center leaving a ½-inch thick shell. Chop the removed portion into approximately ½-inch pieces, place in small bowl. Salt generously both the shell and chopped pieces. Let shell stand about 1 hr., the chopped 30 min., then drain it well, sauté it together with ¼ c. chopped onion, 1 clove minced garlic, 2 T. finely chopped celery in ¼ c. butter or substitute.*

Add   1½ c. soft bread crumbs or substitute, 1½ c. cooked cleaned shrimp—fresh or canned (use small shrimp whole, larger ones may be cut. Save a few whole for garnishing.)—¼ c. minced parsley, ½ tsp. thyme. Spoon into drained eggplant shell and place in a buttered baking dish. Bake at 375° 30–40 min. Eggplant should be fork tender. Sprinkle with paprika and the whole shrimp. Serves 6.

BROILED SCALLOPS OR PRAWNS ORIENTAL
(wheat, milk, and egg free)

This is equally good for scallops or prawns, but the scallops are more unusual. The fish should soak in the marinade 2–3 hrs. The cooking time is only minutes. They are elegant either as an hors d'oeuvres or as an entrée.

Cut scallops into bite-size pieces

---

* Chopped bacon or salt pork may be browned and added with the shrimp and the grease from its cooking substituted for the butter or vegetable shortening.

Put 1½ lbs. fish in bowl large enough to cover with marinade
Mix ½ c. salad or olive oil, ½ cup soy sauce, ½ c. dry sherry
½ tsp. powdered ginger, ¼ tsp. garlic powder
Pour mixture over fish, being sure fish is completely covered.
At cooking time remove fish from marinade, place loosely on
skewers. Set on broiler rack about 2 inches from heat in a preheated broiler. Broil about 5 min., turning at least once and
basting with marinade. Serve immediately. 4–6 servings as an
entrée.

Small filets of white fish can also be used. They are very good
and less expensive. Do not skewer. Broil on a preheated broiler,
turning once.

OYSTERS

Fresh oysters are not always available and in parts of the
country are rare. But the canned whole small oysters can be used
with considerable finesse as a substitute. In some of the larger
chain groceries a very good quality at a reasonable price is
available.

BROILED OYSTERS (wheat, milk, and egg free)

Choose small or medium-sized oysters. Place on a sheet of foil
in a baking dish adjusting size of foil to just hold oysters in a
flat single layer. Sprinkle with a little thyme and terragon or
chervil. Pour dry sherry, chablis, or sauterne over oysters to
about ¼ inch depth. Place 3–4 inches under heat. Broil until
edges curl and they look dry on top. Turn carefully and repeat.
Spoon juice over oysters before serving. Pass any extra juice,
or it may be thickened as a sauce.

OYSTER STUFFED EGGPLANT
(wheat, milk, and egg free)

Prepare as for shrimp stuffed eggplant substituting 1 pt. drained

and chopped oysters of 2 8 oz. tins drained and chopped. Bake
at 375° for 30 min. Serves 6.

SALMON

Salmon has a more pronounced flavor than sole or halibut, but
care must still be taken not to destroy its flavor. As with white
fish steaming, broiling and baking are the superior methods of
cooking, and nothing is more delectable than salmon filets bar-
becued.

STUFFED BAKED SALMON
(wheat, milk, and egg free)

This stuffing adds to the fish without overpowering it. Clean,
scrape scales, wash and pat dry a 4–5 lb. salmon. Salt lightly.
Fill with the following filling:
Break 3–4 slices slightly dry bread or substitute (see page 106)
into small pieces. There should be about 1½ c. bread packed in
measuring cup. Cover with ½ c. sherry and let stand 10 min.
Then press out excess wine.

Sauté in 2 T. butter or bacon grease ¼ c. finely chopped
green pepper, ¼ c. minced onion, ¼ c. finely chopped celery.
Add ¾ c. sliced fresh mushrooms (canned may be substituted)
and 2 T. chopped parsley. Cook about 10 min., then stir in bread
crumbs. Mix well. Stuff lightly into fish. Fasten fish with toothpicks or small skewers and secure with string or heavy thread
lacing.

Rub fish with salt, soft butter or oil. Slices of bacon on top are
optional. Place fish on heavy foil in roaster or baking pan. Pull
foil up around salmon (not airtight) for about half of baking
time, then pull back and complete baking. It can be basted with
lemon juice and stock if needed.

Bake at 350°, allowing 15 min. to the pound. Serve with
lemon wedges or sauce desired.

SMOKED SALMON

Smoked salmon lends itself to a variety of uses ranging from appetizers and salads through entrees for lunch, brunch, or dinner. Lox, the hardest to find, is mildly cured King salmon which will slice very thin and therefore lends itself to fancy sandwiches, fancy filled rolls for appetizers, and the like. The more robust kippered salmon has a much stronger smoke flavor, does not slice well, but is more adaptable. Cut into bite-sized pieces, served with crackers; as hors d'oeuvres; it can be mashed and used in a dip, broken into pieces in a salad or as part of a salad plate, or used in cooked dishes as in the following recipes.

STEAMED KIPPERED SALMON
(wheat, milk, and egg free)

Wrap the desired amount of salmon tightly in foil. Set in steamer, cover, and allow to steam 15–20 min., or sufficient time to heat through. To serve with the fish, melt butter, add lemon juice, a little prepared mustard, and a shake of dill weed. Taste for flavoring; adjust if necessary. The amount is determined by the quantity of fish. If butter must be omitted, serve with plain lemon wedges; caper or dill sauce are optional.

Appetizing accompaniments for this are parsley potatoes and mushrooms and asparagus tips or zucchini.

CREAMED KIPPERED SALMON OR COD
(wheat, milk, and egg free)

To prepare salmon steam as for steamed salmon, break apart, and remove any bones.

Stir into prepared sauce. Serve on mashed potatoes, steamed rice, toast, on in pastry shells.

Where milk is to be eliminated, use Cream Rich as you would milk or half-and-half. (See page 96)

For a pound or little more of salmon make a cream sauce using 2 T. butter, margarine or shortening with butter flavoring.

2 T. flour or substitute, 1 c. half-and-half, ½ tsp. A-1, dash of onion powder, ¼ tsp. prepared mustard; 1 T. chopped capers may be added for caper sauce, or dill weed to taste for dill sauce, or ½ tsp. (or more to taste) curry powder for curry sauce.

PICKLED FISH (wheat, milk, and egg free)

If you like pickled fish this recipe is for you. It is easy, gives variety of fish, and in markets where fresh fish is available is economical. Experiment with any firm, mild, non-oily white fish. Herring is the commercial standby, but try halibut, flounder, smelts, red snapper, trout, or whatever fish is available. Salmon also is delicious but requires about a week to cure instead of several days as for white fish.

The fish must be boned, skinned, and cut into pieces ¼–½ inch thick and 1–3 inches long, depending on intended use. For snacks or hors d'oeuvres smaller pieces are easier to handle— larger ones are better for sandwiches. The prepared fish should be layered loosely with thinly sliced red or white onion (if too tightly packed the marinade cannot do its work) and covered with the following marinade. For approximately 2 lbs. of fish use 1 large onion sliced. In a small pan combine and simmer for 10 min. the following: 1 c. white vinegar, ½ c. dry white wine or 1½ c. wine vinegar, ½ c. mild honey or sugar, 1 tsp. salt, 1 large bay leaf, ¼ tsp. dry mustard, 1 tsp. dill seed.

Cool slightly. Pour over fish and onion in jars. Cover tightly. Store in refrigerator several days before using. This will keep 2–3 weeks.

SAUCES FOR FISH

COURT BOUILLON (egg, milk, wheat and gluten free)

To make fish stock for poaching and as a base for sauces use the court bouillon recipe for cooking prawns (see page 130) and add

1–2 lbs. fish trimmings. (Your butcher or the fish market can readily supply this.) One c. white wine may be substituted for 1 c. water. A carrot and some parsley may be added. Cook gently about 1 hr. Let steep about 1 hr. and then strain.

MUSTARD SAUCE

Melt 3 T. butter or vegetable shortening (see page 97)
Blend in 2 T. flour or substitute (see page 104)
Stir in slowly 1 c. fish stock or chicken broth with 1 T. lemon juice. Cook until thickened. Add ½ tsp. dry mustard, salt and pepper to taste. Blend well. Serve hot.

CAPER SAUCE

Add 1 T. caper or to taste to above recipe.

SHRIMP SAUCE NO. 1

Thicken tomato sauce (see baked red snapper) with 1–2 T. flour or substitute. Add ½ c. shrimp, ½ c. sautéed or canned mushrooms, 2 tsp. capers (optional).

SHRIMP SAUCE NO. 2
(for milk free, see p. 96)

To 2 c. medium white sauce add 1 tsp. A-1 or Worcestershire, ½ tsp. onion powder, ¼ tsp. thyme, ¼ c. dry white wine (optional), ½ c. shrimp.

Substitute cream rich and vegetable shortening for milkless. Use potato or rice flour for wheat substitute.

Sauté 2 T. chopped onion in ¼ c. melted butter or substitute. Blend in ¼ c. flour or substitute and ⅛ tsp. thyme. Gradually add 1 c. chicken broth and 1 c. milk or 1 c. Coffee Rich. Stir and cook until thickened. Add ¼ lb. chopped shrimp fresh or canned. Add salt and pepper to taste. Cook 5 min.

DILL SAUCE (wheat, milk, and egg free)

Make as a white sauce using 6 T. butter, margarine or oil, 6 T. flour or substitute, and 3 c. court bouillon. Or the fat may be eliminated entirely and a flour-and-water paste stirred into the bouillon. Cook over medium heat, stirring until thickened. It should be like a soft custard. Add ½ tsp. dried dill or 2 tsp. fresh chopped, 2 T. sherry (optional) and more salt if needed.

Chicken broth may be substituted for the court bouillon. For this use 1 tsp. onion powder or 2 tsp. grated onion, ¼ tsp. celery salt, ½–¾ tsp. salt, depending on chicken stock, 2 T. lemon juice or sherry, dill as above, pepper to taste.

BEEF

BEEF CURRY WITH RAISINS
(wheat, milk, and egg free)

Sauté ½ c. minced onions (more if desired) in a small amount of shortening.

Add 1 lb. lean ground beef. Cook, stirring frequently, until beef is browned.

Add 1 tsp. curry powder and ½ c. plumped seedless raisins. Salt and pepper to taste. Simmer gently until flavors are blended.

Heap on platter, circle with hot cooked rice. Garnish with fried bananas. 4–6 servings.

EASY CHILI (wheat, milk, and egg free)

Chop 1 onion and 1 clove garlic. Cook until limp and golden in as little shortening as possible.

Add 1 lb. lean ground beef. Cook and stir until all pink is gone. Remove any fat.

Add two 1 lb. cans red beans with tomato sauce, ½ tsp. salt, 1 tsp.–1 T. chili powder or to taste, 1 c. catsup, and a dash of Worcestershire or A-1 sauce. Adjust salt.

Simmer gently a few minutes to blend flavors. Serve plain or heaped over hot cooked rice.

BEEF ROLLS (wheat, milk, and egg free)

Top round steak does very well for this. Pound ½-inch thick steak to ¼-inch thickness and cut into pieces 3–4 inches for individual servings, or 1 large roll can be made. Lay flat in pan or bowl and cover with burgundy, or a mixture of half olive oil and half lemon juice. Leave about 1 hr. (This step is optional.) Then spread flat, put dressing (recipe below) in center of rolls. Roll, fasten with tooth picks, and tie. Brown in oil, butter, or margarine. Add equal parts burgundy and beef stock, plain stock, or tomato juice to ¼ inch depth around rolls. Cover and simmer on top of stove for about 35 min., or bake at 350° about 45 min. or until tender, basting occasionally. Replenish liquid if needed. Remove strings and toothpicks to serve. Pour any remaining juice over them. Surround by extra dressing and serve. 2 lbs. of beef will make 5–6 servings.

The filling can be a typical bread dressing, an ala or Bulgar pilaf, or where wheat is to be avoided a brown rice pilaf with red beans is interesting. To make it, finely chop enough salt pork to make ¼ c. Put on medium heat to brown. Add ½ c. each chopped green pepper, and celery, ¾ c. minced onion. Cook all together several minutes. The salt pork should be thoroughly browned. Add 1 c. brown rice, 1 bay leaf, ¼ tsp. thyme, ¼ tsp. rosemary, 1 T. chopped parsley, 1 tsp. sugar, the solid portion of 1 fresh or canned tomato chopped. Measure amount of liquid recommended on your rice package.

Beef broth (made with bouillon cubes will do) is better than water. Do not add quite all at once. More can be added later if needed, but the rice should not be soggy. Cover and simmer until *not* quite tender. Mix in one 15–16 oz. can of drained kidney beans. Spread mixture on meat. Proceed as above. There will be extra pilaf. Set it aside until shortly before meat is ready. Return it to the heat or put in oven with the meat rolls to finish cooking. Serve separately.

STUFFED MEAT LOAF (wheat, milk, and egg free)

The brown rice pilaf recipe above can also be used as meat-loaf filling. Spread half of prepared meat-loaf mixture (see page 00) in bottom of greased casserole or bread tin, spreading up sides a little. Put layer of filling on top. Cover with remaining meat. Top with tomato sauce seasoned with a little onion powder, rosemary, basil, and lemon juice. Bake as usual.

ASPIC OF BEEF WITH HORSERADISH CREAM
(egg and wheat free)

A tasty, nourishing, summer or cold buffet entrée. Allow at least two days. Proportions can be cut for smaller loaf. Start with about 8 lbs. well-marbled or larded top sirloin and 1 cracked veal knuckle. Marinate 24 hrs. in 1¾ c. orange juice and ⅓ c. wine vinegar, or ⅓ c. Chablis for part of orange juice. Turn meat several times.

Next day remove meat, save marinade. Rub meat with mixture of 2 tsp. salt, ¼ c. flour or substitute. (see page 104)

Brown in heavy pot on all sides in 2 T. oil. Remove all excess drippings. Add to marinade 1 whole carrot, 1 tsp. powdered onion, few sprigs parsley, few celery tops, 2 cloves garlic, and 3 T. prepared horseradish. Season with 1 T. salt, 1 tsp. thyme, ½ tsp. marjoram, pepper if desired. Pour over meat in Dutch oven. Tuck the cracked veal knuckle around meat and cover tightly. Simmer 4–5 hours or until tender. Remove meat and knuckle. Cool.

Strain the broth through several thicknesses of cheesecloth and chill. Skim off all the fat when solidified. When meat has completely cooled, trim off outer fat and slice meat very thin crosswise. Cut into pieces to fit a 9 × 5 × 3-inch pan or mold. Heat the broth until unjelled. When it is cool, add 1 c. yogurt, ¼ –½ c. horseradish depending on the strength of the horseradish, 3 T. white wine vinegar, 2 T. sugar, and ½ tsp. salt. Soften 1 envelope unflavored gelatin in ¼ c. cold water. Dissolve over hot water. Stir in a bit of the yogurt-broth mixture, then add to remainder of mixture. Mix well, chill until partially thickened like whipped cream. This is important. Pour enough in mold to cover bottom and chill until set.

Dip each slice of meat in the mixture and place perpendicularly in the pan (like a loaf of bread) until pan is filled. Sauce must be set enough to stick to meat. Fill in any cavities with extra meat and pour remaining sauce carefully over all. Chill overnight or until set. Unmold and garnish with cucumbers and radish slices or tomato slices.

Serve with extra horseradish sauce on side if you wish. Mix together 1 c. yogurt, ½ c. prepared horseradish, 1 T. sugar, 4–5 T. vinegar, salt and pepper to taste.

BARBECUED BEEF—SHORT RIBS
(wheat, milk, and egg free)

Select 3–4 lbs. meaty ribs. Cut into serving-size pieces. Sprinkle with salt and pepper. Place in roaster and cover with two sliced onions.

Cover with a sauce made by combining 2 T. vinegar, 2 T. Worcestershire sauce, 1 T. salt, 1 tsp. paprika, ½ tsp. pepper, 1 tsp. chili powder (optional) ¾ c. catsup, and ¾ c. water. Pour over meat. Cover and bake at 350° for 1½ hrs. or until tender. Baste occasionally turning ribs once or twice. Remove cover from roaster during last 15 min. to brown ribs. Serves 6.

OLD-FASHIONED BEEF STEW
(wheat, milk, and egg free)

Allow 3 hrs.

Preheat a Dutch oven or kettle, throw in a little suet pulled into little chunks, and when it melts enough to cover the bottom of the kettle and splatters put in about 2 lbs. beef stew meat, trimmed and cut into uniform pieces. Brown well on all sides. This takes about 20 min.

Then add 4 c. boiling liquid. It may be broth made with beef cubes, stock, or water. Add 1 clove garlic minced, 1 medium-size onion chopped, 2 bay leaves, 1 T. salt, ½ tsp. pepper, ½ tsp. paprika, dash of powdered allspice or cloves, 1 tsp. lemon juice, 1tsp. A-1 sauce, and 1tsp. sugar.

Cover pot and reduce heat. Shake pot occasionally so the meat won't stick. Add liquid if necessary but it is not to be soup.

After 2½ hrs. add 1 bunch tender young carrots scraped and quartered, some small white boiling onions, and quartered potatoes. When meat and vegetables are tender, remove them from the liquid to a casserole.

Mix 4 T. flour or substitute (see page 104) with a little water to make a paste. Add to meat liquid slowly. Blend thoroughly, stir until thickened. Then cook over low heat for 5 minutes, stirring constantly. Add about ¼ c. catsup, a few drops of kitchen bouquet (optional). Thin to desired consistency if necessary. Adjust seasoning. Just before removing from heat stir in a small glass of sherry. Pour over meat and serve immediately.

SPICED FLANK STEAK
(wheat, milk, and egg free)

Combine ⅓ c. vinegar, 2 tsp. salt, 2 T. sugar, ½ tsp. cloves, ¾ tsp. cinnamon, 1 bay leaf, broken, ½ tsp. pepper. Heat and let cool. Put a flank steak (about 1¼ lbs.) in a bowl and cover with the marinade. Refrigerate 8 hours or more. Turn several times.

Mix 1 tsp. chopped parsley, salt and 2 T. fat with 1 c. cooked rice. Chopped bacon or mushrooms may be added (optional). Remove steak from marinade, spread with cooked rice. Roll and tie meat. Brown in a little shortening with 1 sliced onion. Almost cover with hot bouillon. Cover and simmer for 2 hours or until meat is tender. Remove to hot platter. Thicken remaining liquid for gravy. Serves four.

SPAGHETTI MEAT SAUCE
(milk, egg and wheat free)

Allow 3–4 hours for sauce to cook.

In a large pot, sauté 1 large chopped onion and 1 clove chopped garlic in 3–4 T. olive oil until golden. Add two cans tomato paste, two No. 2½ tins canned tomatoes whirled in the blender or put through food mill. Seeds should be removed. Add 1 bay leaf, 1 tsp. rosemary, ½ tsp. oregano, ½ tsp. basil, 2 slices lemon, ½ tsp. Accent, about 1 T. salt, 1 tsp. sugar. Cover and simmer about 3 hrs., stirring occasionally. Add some broth water if becomes too thick.

Rub frying pan with lightly greased pastry brush so as to prevent meat sticking. Over medium heat cook just until all pink is gone 1½–2 lbs. ground round depending on leanness. Remove excess fat. Salt meat to taste. Add to meat sauce and continue simmering about 1 hr. more, stirring occasionally. Add water, broth, or Burgundy wine if needs any thinning. If too thin, simmer with pot uncovered until it boils down to right consistency. Adjust seasoning.

Serve over spaghetti which has been cooked in lots of water just until tender. Sprinkle with fresh-grated Parmesan cheese. Cornbread* or rice may be substituted for the spaghetti for wheatless menus.

CORNED BEEF (egg, milk, and gluten free)

Pick a well-trimmed, lean, top-quality corned brisket or round of beef. The quality of the meat determines the end results.

To cook: Put beef in a large kettle. Cover with cold water. Bring water to a boil, drain it off, rinse meat free of all scum. Repeat the boiling and draining three times in all. Then cover with cold water once more. Add 1 peeled whole onion, 1 stalk of celery, 1 bay leaf, 6 peppercorns, and a piece of lean-streaked salt pork. Bring to a boil, reduce heat. Simmer gently until beef is fork tender, 3–4 hours depending on size and cut of beef. Skim off fat. Remove part of stock if vegetables are to be boiled with meat. Save stock for soup. Try and save some meat for:

REUBEN SANDWICHES (wheat, milk, and egg free)

Use rye, pumpernickel, or 100 percent rye (for wheat free) bread.

---
* See page 40.

Slice hot or cold corned beef very thin. Put generous amounts on first slice of bread or toast. Heap with sauerkraut (hot or cold), top with slices of Swiss cheese. Mustard or catsup optional. Top with second slice of bread. Feast!

CORNED BEEF SLICES
(egg, milk, and gluten free)

Canned corn beef may be used for this. Chill thoroughly. Cut into ¼-inch slices. Spread both sides with prepared mustard. Dip slices into cornmeal until well coated. In a heavy frying pan over medium heat melt enough butter or shortening to cover bottom of pan. Fry slices until golden brown. Turn and repeat. Allow about 10 min. for cooking. Garnish with orange slices.

TAMALE CASSEROLE WITH KIDNEY BEAN SAUCE
(wheat, milk, and egg free)

A complete meal with just a tossed salad. Economical, easy to prepare and can be made ahead and refrigerated or frozen. Adjust cooking time accordingly.

You will need 5 c. beef broth, canned, made from bouillon cubes, or homemade.

Mix 1 c. cold broth with 1¼ c. yellow cornmeal until completely moistened. (This helps prevent lumping of the mush.) Melt 1 T. butter or shortening in the remaining 4 c. of boiling broth. Slowly stir in the moistened cornmeal and stir until thick and smooth. Place pan over boiling water (double boiler) and cook about 40 min., stirring occasionally. While this is cooking, prepare meat mixture.

Chop fine 1 green pepper, 1 medium onion, 1 clove garlic. Dice 1 inch square salt pork. Cook until fat is crispy. Remove from pan. Add cooking oil if necessary to make 2 T. Add chopped vegetables and cook until tender but not brown.

Add 1¼ lb. lean ground beef (1½ lb. if not lean). Cook, stirring, until meat is no longer pink. Drain off any excess fat. Add salt pork.

To ⅔ c. tomato puree add 2 T. flour or substitute (see page 104), ½ tsp. sugar, 1 tsp. salt, 1–3 tsp. chili powder, depending on the variety and your taste, 6–8 chopped ripe olives (optional). Add to beef, mix well. Turn down heat, cover, and let simmer while you go back to the cornmeal. When it is cooked add ¼ c. finely chopped parsley and salt to taste. Pour half of the cornmeal into a well-greased casserole, smoothing it out and up the sides a little. Taste the meat mixture. Adjust any seasoning. Pour over cornmeal in casserole and cover with remaining cornmeal.

Allow 1 hr. for baking for unfrozen—longer if frozen. Bake covered at 350°. About 20 min. before it is done remove cover and continue baking. Just before serving, dot with butter or substitute and put under broiler to brown lightly. Serve with Kidney Bean Sauce.

KIDNEY BEAN SAUCE

This is best made in advance and reheated in order to give the flavors a chance to blend.

Sauté ¼ c. chopped onion and 1 clove chopped garlic in 1½ T. oil until golden. Add one 15–16 oz. can kidney beans, 1 8-oz. can tomato sauce, 1–2 tsp. chili powder, ¾ tsp. oregano, ½ tsp. paprika, ⅛ tsp. powdered cloves, ½ tsp. salt, ⅛ tsp. sugar and pepper to taste. Bring to a boil. Simmer a few minutes but do not break or mash beans. Taste for seasoning and adjust if needed. Put into bowl and pass separately.

POLYNESIAN MEAT BALLS
(wheat, milk, and egg free)

Use lean ground beef. Shape into small meat balls, allowing 4–6 per serving. Place in a single layer in a bowl. Add a little powdered ginger and onion salt to enough soy sauce to partially cover meat balls. Pour over meat balls, turn balls in marinade until they have absorbed all the sauce they will. Lift carefully and brown gently in lightly greased skillet. Serve on hot brown rice.

These are also excellent as an hors d'oeuvre. Simply insert a toothpick to serve.

BUTA MANJU—JAPANESE STEAMED MEAT DUMPLINGS
(egg and milk free)

The Japanese steam these dumplings and serve them either hot or cold as one of the many courses comprising a dinner. For us they can replace a sandwich, be combined with another entree, or be made as suggested below for a complete entree.

To make 12 dumplings mix together and knead 8 min. 1 pkg. dry yeast, 3¼ c. sifted flour, 3 T. sugar, 3 T. oil, and 1 c. water.

Put in oiled bowl, cover, and let double in bulk. Punch down once, let rise again. Then on a floured board or pastry cloth shape dough into a roll. Cut into 12 pieces. Roll each piece until about 6 inches in diameter.

Put about 1 T. filling (recipe below) on each circle, pull edges together tightly to make a ball. Put a circle of waxed paper about 3 inches in diameter over gathered seam. Turn so that paper is on the bottom. Let rise 1 hr. Steam 10 min.

Filling: Mix together about ½ lb. ground beef and pork, 1 finely chopped onion plus 1 green onion, top included, 3–4 big dry mushrooms which have been soaked in very mild vinegar and a little sugar (chopped fresh or canned can be substituted), chopped, and 1 small grated carrot.

Cook in frying pan, stirring, until meat is cooked and onion is soft. Salt to taste.

Variations for Buta Manju: The choice of meats can be varied. Also the seasoning. The Japanese use large quantities of onion. Less may be used is desired.

Baked Dumplings: These dumplings, baked and served with a meat sauce, make a delightful entree for a hearty luncheon or a dinner. Make at least double the recipe for filling. Roll dough into larger circles or put as much more filling as possible in each and still make a tight seal. Instead of steaming, bake at 375° about 25 min. or until lightly browned. Serve 2–3 for a dinner entree covered with the following meat sauce.

Dilute canned cream of mushroom soup half as much as for

soup with milk or half-and-half. Add extra meat filling and more mushrooms. Serve very hot.

For milkless use a homemade soup.

VEAL

Veal must be treated with as much caution as many varieties of fish. Its flavor is so delicate it is easily overwhelmed.

VEAL SCALLOPPINI DELUXE
(wheat, milk, and egg free)

Veal round gives the nicest looking pieces, but shoulder steak tastes almost as good. For 6–8 servings pound 2 lbs. veal ⅛–¼-inch (not more) thickness. For shoulder steak some of the connective tissue may need to be removed to release the meat. Cut into serving-size pieces. Dredge in wheat or potato flour with salt and pepper added. Fry slowly in salad or olive oil until lightly browned. Remove to Dutch oven, or if using an electric fry pan remove to warm plate temporarily.

Turn down heat. Add 2 c. Chablis or dry Sauterne mixed with 1 tsp. mei yen, ½ tsp. onion powder, ¼ tsp. rosemary, ¼ tsp. thyme (too much thyme gives bitter flavor), ½ tsp. salt.

Let sizzle in pan 1 min., return meat to pan. Cover and let simmer 45 min. to 1 hr. Sliced mushrooms may be added about 20 min. before serving time.

Chicken broth may be substituted for the wine but the flavor is not the same.

VEAL PORKOLT OR PAPRIKAS
(wheat and egg free)

Sauté 2 chopped onions in 3 T. shortening until golden brown. Add 1 tsp. paprika and cook 1 min. Lift out onion. Add 2 lbs. diced veal to shortening. Sear. Shoulder does nicely. When lightly brown return onions. Add ½ tsp. salt and little water. Cook slowly 1½ hrs. or until tender. Add little hot water from time to time but not enough to steam or boil.

Add 1 c. sour cream and few drops of lemon juice 1 min. before serving (or ½ c. undiluted evaporated milk and 1 T. lemon juice). Circle with mashed potatoes.

BAKED VEAL GOULASH
(wheat, milk, and egg free)

Cube and fry out in skillet ¼ lb. salt pork. Remove pork and put into a large casserole.

Chop and brown 1 large onion in pork fat together with 1–1½ lb. cubed veal. Shoulder may be used. Remove to casserole. To fat left in skillet add most of 4 c. tomato juice, 1 tsp. salt, 3 bay leaves, ¼ tsp. pepper, 1 tsp. paprika. Mix 3 T. flour or substitute with remaining liquid, stir in gradually. Cook slowly stirring until slightly thickened. Add to meat and onions. Bake at 350° 1½ hrs. Add 6 small carrots cut in sections, and 6 small potatoes cut in pieces. Add liquid if necessary. Bake about 1 hr. more or until meat is tender and vegetables are cooked. 6 servings.

VEAL ROAST SEASONING

This is very simple and gives that complete extra something to the flavor of the veal.

Combine 1 T. olive oil, 1 T. dry sherry, 1 tsp. mei yen, ½ tsp. onion powder, 1 tsp. fresh rosemary or ¼ tsp. dried, ¼ tsp. thyme, 1 tsp. salt, parsley. Spoon part over roast and rub in before baking. Baste with remainder as it cooks.

VEAL SAUTÉ (wheat, milk, and egg free)

Allow 1 lb. trimmed veal, cut into thin strips (not chunks) for 3–4 servings. The better the cut of veal the better the result; however, stew meat can be used if it is carefully trimmed and allowed to cook longer.

Gently brown prepared veal in 2 T. olive oil. Sprinkle on ½ tsp. onion powder, ½ tsp. rosemary, ½ tsp basil, ¼ tsp. Accent and ¼ tsp. thyme. Add a thin slice of lemon or a little grated rind. Stir meat until seasonings are well distributed. Add about ¼ c. liquid—dry sherry and stock in equal proportions are best. There should be just enough to cover the bottom of the pan. This is not a stew. Add more as it cooks if necessary. Cover pan and simmer—don't boil—until meat is tender, 15–20 min. for the tender cuts. Stir occasionally. Add salt to taste and adjust other seasonings if necessary. The meat should be moist and tender. Spoon any pan juice over meat as it is served. Serve on noodles, spaghetti or rice. Pass freshly grated Parmesan cheese (omit for milkless).

STUFFED VEAL STEAK ROLL
(wheat, milk, and egg free)

In many recipes for veal birds and rolls the filling overwhelms the veal until the veal flavor is lost. This recipe enhances the veal flavor. One veal round steak will make 3 average servings.

Cut off all connective tissue which confines meat. Lay a ½-inch-thick steak between double thicknesses of waxed paper and with a small mallet pound veal to ¼ inch thickness.

Mix ingredients for veal roast seasoning. Spread most of it onto steak. Let stand while preparing filling.

Follow cooking directions on a 6-oz. package of white and wild rice. (Plain rice may be substituted.) While it is cooking chop very fine 1 medium-size piece of celery, ¼ medium-size green pepper, about 6 water chestnuts (optional), 1 T. finely chopped green onion, ¼ c. chopped mushrooms (optional). Cook until limp in 3–4 T. olive oil. Add ¼ tsp. salt, a dash of crushed basil and rosemary. Turn down heat. Stir in 2 tsp. dry sherry (optional) and add 1½ c. of the cooked rice. Mix all together. Taste and adjust seasoning.

Spread rice mixture onto veal steak, so that steak will roll around it. Roll, fasten with toothpicks or small skewers and tie with thread if necessary. Brown roll on all sides in about 2 T. olive oil. Pour remaining marinade on top. Add ¼ c. chicken stock or chicken stock and sherry to pan. Cover and simmer for about 30 min. or until tender. Baste occasionally as it cooks; add more chicken stock if necessary.

At serving time remove to warm platter, remove strings and toothpicks. Spoon any remaining drippings over meat, surround with remaining rice which has been kept hot.

The proportions may be doubled or increased as desired, and the meat may be cut into individual serving sizes for veal birds. Lovely served with honey-glazed baby carrots.

LAMB

BARBECUED OR BROILED BONED LEG OF LAMB

Allow at least 24 hrs.—2 days is better—for lamb to absorb flavors of marinade. Unless you are handy at butchering have your butcher bone a leg of lamb so that it will lie as flat as possible. It is to be cooked flat, so do not roll or tie. (Save the bones for later use.) Place in a large bowl or pan. For the marinade combine 1 crushed or finely minced clove of garlic. ⅔ c. minced onion, 1 tsp. salt, ½ tsp. oregano, ½ tsp. basil, ½ tsp. rosemary, ¼ tsp. chervil or tarragon, 1 crushed bay leaf, 1 c. oil and vinegar French dressing (preferably red wine vinegar) or add 2 T. dry red wine. Heat on stove just until very hot to marry flavors. Cool and pour over meat. Let it absorb all the goodness for 24 hrs. at least, or 2 days if possible. Turn meat several times.

For barbecueing, the easiest method is to place meat inside a wire rack and lock it firmly in place. Cook 45 min. to 1 hr., turning frequently and basting with the marinade.

To broil: Place meat fat side up on broiler pan, brush well with marinade, broil about 4 inches from heat about 10 min. or until the fat turns golden brown. Turn meat, baste, and broil 10 min. or until this side is browned. Then set oven control at

450° and bake 30–35 min. Turn fat side up again and bake another 5 min.

This produces a well-done exterior and a slightly pinkish inside, juicy, and delectable. If you must, cook it longer for better done inside.

PLUM GLAZED LEG OF LAMB
(wheat, milk, and egg free)

Trim any excess fat from a medium-size leg of lamb. Rub meat with salt and pepper and ½ tsp. onion powder. Roast meat at 400° about 25 min. or until meat is browned. Reduce heat to 300°. Drain off any accumulated fat in roasting pan. Pour 1 c. chicken broth into pan and cook additional 1–1½ hrs., basting occasionally. Mix together ¾ c. plum jelly or jam which has been put through food mill or blender and strained, 1½ tsp. dry mustard, ½ tsp. powdered ginger, and 1 tsp. soy sauce. Thirty min. before roast is done, spread mixture over meat and baste as needed. If you use a meat thermometer it should read 145° for rare, 160° for medium, and 175° for well done. A roast that is to be juicy must not be overdone.

SAVORY LAMB (wheat, milk, and egg free)

A tasty way to use leftover cooked lamb. Proportions are adjustable to fit the supplies and the demand. The basic recipe:

Peel and dice enough raw eggplant to make about 2 c. of ½-inch cubes. Place in bowl and salt well. Slowly brown 3–4 slices of thick bacon or equivalent of salt pork. Lift out of skillet. You will need about 3 T. fat remaining. Adjust as necessary. To this add the drained eggplant, ¼ c. chopped green onion, ¼ c. diced green pepper, 1 clove minced garlic. Cook together 5 min. Add 2 c. diced lean cooked lamb. Strain juice from 1 No. 2 can of stewed tomatoes and add solids. (Chopped fresh tomatoes may be used or plain canned tomatoes. For these add a little basil, rosemary, thyme, and bay leaf.) Cover and let simmer gently

5–10 min. If more moisture is needed add some tomato liquid. Salt and pepper to taste. Serve with rice. Yield: 3–4 servings.

GRAPE LEAF ROLLS WITH LAMB
(wheat, milk, and egg free)

Either bottled or fresh grape leaves may be used. Wash fresh ones in hot water. Drain either fresh or bottled. Spread leaves flat with underside up. Cut off stem ends. Roll from that end after filling is in place. Use 2–3 tsp. filling depending on size of leaf. Wrap in ends of leaf so meat is completely enfolded. The rolls are quite small. Allow 2–3 per serving.

Filling for approximately 2 dozen rolls:

Combine 1 lb. uncooked lean ground lamb, 1 T. finely chopped onion, ¾ tsp. salt, pepper to taste. Place rolls in 1½-qt. casserole or pan.

Combine 1 8 oz. can tomato sauce, 2 T. lemon juice, ¼ tsp. salt. Pour over rolls. Cover. Bake at 350° about 50 min. Uncover and bake 10 min. more. Serve with slices of lemon on brown rice, or if wheat is permissible on ala or bulgar.

SHISH KEBOB (wheat, milk, and egg free)

Use boned leg of lamb. The bone is important for the marinade. Separate the bone at the joint so it will fit into a smaller pan. Add 2–3 c. water. Bring slowly to a boil. Skim. Add ½ tsp. salt, ½ tsp. each rosemary and basil, ¼ tsp. oregano, ½ tsp. onion powder or 1 T. minced onion, ¼ tsp. each of thyme and garlic powder. Simmer an hour or so. Liquid should be reduced about half. Add ½ c. red wine, a slice of lemon. Set aside to cool. Then pour over lamb which has been cut into pieces for skewering. Soak lamb in marinade 3–4 hrs., turning meat occasionally. Place on skewers either alone or in combinations of your choice. Small bottled onions, slices of green pepper, pieces of bacon, eggplant or little tomatoes, mushrooms or pineapple chunks are all good. Cook either on the barbecue or place skewers on broiler rack and broil about 4 inches from heat until nicely browned, turn and brown other side basting with marinade as they cook. The time will depend on how well done you wish them.

TANTALIZING LAMB CHOPS
(wheat, milk, and egg free)

Loin chops make this very gourmet, but shoulder chops are very good eating fixed this way.

Brown desired number of chops in hot fat. Season with salt and pepper. Remove any excess fat. Spread just a whisper of prepared mustard on each chop. Top with a green pepper ring, a slice of onion, and a slice of lemon. Pour tomato juice around chops. Cover and simmer until tender basting occasionally for 1-1½ hrs. Or, the chops may be transferred to a baking dish after browning and baked, covered, at 350° until tender.

ARMENIAN MEAT PASTRY
(eggless and milkless)

This is similar to Greek pastry but, unlike most European and Oriental recipes, it has no eggs. Refrigerator biscuits can be rolled very thin and substituted for the yeast dough given here.

Dough:
Dissolve 1 pkg. yeast in ¾ c. warm water
Add ½ tsp. sugar, 1 tsp. salt, ¼ c. salad oil
Stir in 2–2¼ c. sifted flour.

Dough should be soft. Lift onto lightly floured pastry cloth, oil hands, and knead 12–15 min. Put into oiled bowl turning to oil top. Cover. Let rise 2–3 hrs. in a warm place or until dough is more than doubled in bulk. Shortly before dough is ready, mix meat mixture.

Mix together in bowl 1 lb. ground lean lamb, 1 c. finely chopped onion, ¼ c. chopped parsley, ¼ c. chopped green pepper, 1 tsp. chopped fresh mint leaves or ½ tsp. dried, ½ clove garlic chopped, (optional), ½ small can tomato paste, ¾ c. whole canned tomatoes, well drained, 1½–2 tsp. salt, pepper to taste.

Do not precook. Mixture must be dry or juice will run during baking.

When dough is ready, punch down, place on lightly floured pastry cloth. Divide into 12 balls. Roll in hands to shape if necessary. Let dough rest for 10 min., then roll out each piece until about 6 inches in diameter. Place on greased cookie sheet as rolled. Cover each piece with a thin layer of the meat mixture. Bake at 450 ° for 15 min. or until done. Serve hot. Two of these are sufficient for an entrée. Small ones may be served as hors d'oeuvres.

Variations: Other meat mixtures may be substituted for the lamb.

CHICKEN

MACADAMIA CHICKEN (wheat, milk, and egg free)

Pat chicken pieces dry. Place desired number of pieces of breasts and thighs, or other parts, in roaster. Cover with cream of chicken soup, adding ¼ c. sherry to each can. For milkless and wheatless, use homemade soup—but it must be thick. (See soups.) Do not salt. Sprinkle top with macadamia nuts (they are salty), or almonds may be substituted, and bake uncovered at 300° 2–2½ hrs.

OVEN FRIED CHICKEN
(wheat, milk, and egg free)

Grate peel from 1 large lemon. Cut in half.

Combine juice of ½ lemon (2–3 T.), ½ c. melted butter, margarine, or salad oil, ½ tsp. each of paprika, dry mustard, dill weed, grated lemon rind, and 1 tsp. salt in baking dish.

Cut a 2½–3 lb. broiler fryer in pieces or use breasts and thighs if desired. Have chicken at room temperature before dipping. Rub well with remaining half lemon, then dip in butter mixture. Shake in sack of ⅓–½ c. flour or potato flour until lightly coated. (Chicken may also be cooked without flour dip.) All the butter mixture should be used when chicken is all dipped. If not, remove excess. Place chicken skin side down, not overlapping in baking dish.

Bake at 375° 35 min. Turn pieces and continue baking 35–40 min. or until chicken is tender and browned. Serve immediately. Also good cold.

PORK

BAKED SPARE RIBS
(milk, wheat, and egg free)

For finger food as an appetizer use small ribs cut in finger-size pieces. Marinate about 1 hr.

For an entree use country-style meaty ribs cut in serving-size portions or into single ribs as desired. Marinate at least 4–5 hrs., turning occasionally in the marinade.

Bake small ribs at 425° 30–40 min., turning once and basting with marinade several times as they cook.

Bake country-style ribs at 400° 45–55 min. or until done. Turn and baste as for small ribs.

For marinade for 4½ lbs. ribs combine 2 tsp. ginger, 1 tsp. garlic powder, ½ c. honey, ½ c. soy sauce, ¼ c. mild vinegar, ¼ c. dry white wine (or use ½ c. wine vinegar), ½ c. Triple Sec, 1 c. crushed pineapple, 1 thinly sliced large lemon. Yield: 6–8 servings.

PORK CHOPS IN PLUM CURRY SAUCE
(wheat, milk, and egg free)

For 4 large loin chops combine:

1 tsp. powdered onion, ¾ tsp. curry powder, 2 tsp. mei yen

1 tsp. grated orange rind, ¼ c. plum preserves

Stir in 2 T. lime or lemon juice and 1 c. water.

Trim excess fat from chops. Render one piece in skillet, remove, and slowly brown chops on both sides. Cover with sauce stirring it into pan juices. Cover tightly and simmer about 1 hr. or until chops are tender and well glazed. Remove to warm platter. Remove any excess fat from pan. Thicken juices with 1 tsp. cornstarch mixed with small amount of water. Pour over hot chops. Serve immediately. Pork steaks or shoulder chops may be substituted for loin chops.

MANDARIN SWEET SOUR PORK
(milk, wheat, and egg free)

This is an especially pleasing way to use left over pork from a roast.

Trim fat from meat and cut into ½-inch slices and then into pieces about 1 in. long and ¼–½ in. wide. Set aside while preparing sauce.

For 2–3 c. prepared meat combine 2 T. brown sugar, 1 T. cornstarch, ½ tsp. salt, ⅛–¼ tsp. ginger, and ½ tsp. onion powder. Stir in ¼ c. mild vinegar, 1 T. soy sauce, and ½ c. pineapple juice. If taken from crushed pineapple the fruit can be added with the meat. This is optional. Cook, stirring, over medium heat until sauce is thick and clear. Add meat and allow to warm through. Serve with rice.

To make a more festive dish and also stretch the meat add to the sauce with the meat and let simmer together ¼ c. diced onion (omit onion powder above), and ⅓ c. diced green pepper which have been precooked in a small amount of water for 5 min., ½ can sliced water chestnuts, and ½ c. sliced mushrooms. (Dried Japanese mushrooms soaked in a mild sugar and vinegar water and thinly sliced are delicious here, but plain fresh or canned may be used.)

ORIENTAL TENDERLOIN
(wheat, milk, and egg free)

Figure 3–4 servings per lb. For the marinade for one loin combine: ⅛ tsp. ginger, 2 T. honey, 2 T. sherry, 1 T. soy sauce and ⅓ c. chicken broth or consommé. Marinate 3–4 hrs. Remove to roasting dish or pan and bake at 400° about 35–40 min., turning once and basting frequently as it roasts to prevent it drying out. Serve with individual servings of mustard and toasted sesame seed for dipping.

To make an Oriental dinner proceed as above, but 15 min. before meat is ready, sauté in 2 T. butter or shortening over medium heat ¼ c. chopped green onions and 1 medium-size green pepper cut in ¼ in. strips. Add 2 c. fresh bean sprouts (canned may be used but add later), ½ c. sliced water chestnuts, 1 c. Chinese pea pods. Add remaining marinade. Mix well. Cover and cook over moderate heat 5–10 min. Vegetables should be crispy. Serve with hot rice and additional soy sauce.

ORIENTAL PORK LOIN
(wheat, milk, and egg free)

To use the whole loin have your butcher (or do it yourself) bone, roll, and tie a 4–6 lb. roast. Double or triple the amount of marinade. (See above.) With a large piece of heavy foil make a boat like bowl to come up the sides of your roaster. Put meat in bowl and pull foil up around meat as far as possible. Pour in marinade. Let stand 10–12 hrs. or overnight. Either baste or turn roast several times. Before cooking let excess marinade drip off.

This is elegant done on a rotisserie either in the oven or over the coals of the barbecue. Let cook at 350° or as near as possible to maintain on the barbecue for approximately 4 hrs. or 35–40 min. per lb. During the last ½ hr. baste frequently with the remaining marinade. The internal temperature should reach 180–185° if you use a meat thermometer.

It can be baked also but put meat on a rack to prevent glaze from sticking to and charring meat. 8–12 serv.

BAKED LINK SAUSAGE WITH APPLES
(wheat, milk, and egg free)

A special of my mother's which has always been and still is a favorite at my house.

Allow 4–6 link sausages per serving. Brown sausages lightly in large skillet removing all excess grease.

Fill the casserole of your choice nearly full of sliced tart apples. Salt lightly, sprinkle generously with brown sugar. Top with sausages. Cover with foil or lid. Bake at 350–375° until apples are almost tender. Uncover and let sausages brown as apples finish cooking.

Lovely served with baked potatoes or baked squash, which can be cooked in the same oven.

HAM

HAM À LA GINGER ALE
(wheat, milk, and egg free)

Wrap a piece of heavy foil around ham, leaving an opening at top. Place in roasting pan. Pour ginger ale around ham in foil about halfway up ham. Bake according to directions for size and type of ham. A half hr. before ham is done remove from oven, open up foil, remove rind from ham, score if desired, pat on mixture of brown sugar and dry mustard using ¾ c. sugar to 1 tsp. mustard moistened slightly with ginger ale from the pan. Return to oven and finish baking.

BROILED HAM ROLLS
(wheat, milk, and egg free)

Allow one thin slice ham per serving. Spread with apple butter or orange marmalade. Place ½ peeled banana cut lengthwise on each slice. Roll and fasten with a toothpick. Brush with melted butter or shortening. Broil 4–5 inches from heat until heated through and nicely browned.

HAM SLICES CRANBERRY

A festive alternative to fowl for the holiday season. Mix 2 c. raw cranberries with 1 c. honey. Place a thick slice of ham in baking dish. Spread with cranberry mix. Top with second slice of ham, scored and studded with cloves if desired. Bake at 325°

about 1 hr. for tenderized or precooked ham. Baste frequently with pan juices. Garnish with cranberries.

To serve with baked yams or bananas, cook at 350° a shorter time.

HAM WITH CHERRIES
(wheat, milk, and egg free)

When cranberries are not in season try ham with cherries. This works equally well with one thick slice.

Empty contents of 1 can of tart red cherries into dish. Add a drop or two of red coloring and let sit till cherries absorb some of the color. Drain juice. There should be approximately ¾ c. juice to 1 c. cherries. In a small saucepan thicken the cherry juice with a mixture of 3 T. sugar and 1 T. cornstarch. Add ½ tsp. cinnamon and ⅛ tsp. each of cloves and ginger.

Pour over ham. Bake at 350° about 1 hr.

HAM LOAF WITH SWEET SOUR SAUCE
(wheat, milk, and egg free)

This makes quite a sweet flavored loaf.

Combine 1½ lb. ground ham, ¾ lb. fresh lean pork, and 3 c. cornflakes. Shape into one large or individual sized loaves. Put into baking pan.

Combine 1 c. brown sugar, 1 tsp. dry mustard, ¼ c. vinegar, and ¾ c. water or part orange or pineapple juice. Bring to a boil. Boil 2 min. Drizzle about half over loaf before cooking. Add remaining during cooking basting frequently. Bake at 350° for 1–1½ hrs.

For gluten free, use gluten free cereal or about ⅔ c. gluten free bread or corn bread crumbs.

POTATO HAM LOAF
(wheat, milk, and egg free)

Combine 1½ lbs. ground ham and ½ lb. lean ground fresh pork with 1 c. plain mashed potatoes. Potato flakes are fine for this. For milkless, eliminate the milk and use ¼ c. vinegar as part of the mixing water. Orange or pineapple juice may also replace water. To use boiled potatoes, mash with or without milk and use part vinegar. Add 2 tsp. prepared mustard 2 T. brown sugar ¼ tsp. ginger. Mix well. Shape into loaf and place in bread pan or casserole. Bake at 350° for 1½ hrs.

Serve with sauce of choice.

SAUCES FOR HAM
(wheat, milk, and egg free)

Currant Sauce: Beat together until smooth one 10–12 oz. jar of currant jelly, 3 T. mild vinegar and 1 T. prepared mustard. Part of this may be used as a glaze during cooking; the remainder served as a separate sauce.

Currant and Cranberry Sauce: To the currant sauce above add a 1 lb. can of whole cranberry sauce and 2 T. finely chopped mint. Blend all together.

Raisin Sauce: Mix together ⅓ c. brown sugar, 1½ T. cornstarch and 1 c. liquid. This may be cider, ¼ c. vinegar and ¾ c. water or orange or apple juice, or part sherry. Cook until thickened. Add ⅓–¼ c. plumped raisins. Serve hot.

Marmalade Glaze: Combine ¾ c. marmalade, 1 tsp. dry mustard, and ¼ tsp. ginger. Mix well.

GLAZED CANADIAN BACON
(wheat, milk, and egg free)

For 8–12 servings buy a 2 lb. piece of ready to eat Canadian bacon. Leave the transparent wrapping on it. Place in a shallow baking pan or dish. Bake at 325° for 30 min. Remove from oven, remove wrapper, and stud with cloves (optional). Mix ½ c. brown sugar and ⅓ c. orange juice. Pour over top. Bake another 30 min., basting frequently. To serve slice very thin. Pass drippings in a bowl.

For 4–6 servings, slice 1 lb. into ¼-inch slices. Place in single layer in baking dish. Cover with glaze using above or glaze for Pork Oriental (page 156). Bake at 325° 25–30 min.

Part III
Vegetables and Soups

5
Egg, Milk, Wheat
and Gluten-Free

The vegetable recipes below will serve to give you some ideas on how to make all vegetables more savory.

The soup recipes will be helpful where commercially canned soups, many of which contain wheat or milk—plain or hydrolized—cannot be used.

Also see Chapter 4 page 125, for suggested substitutions for egg dips and binders. Vegetables can be treated in the same manner as meats and fish.

BAKED PARSNIPS IN CREAM
(wheat, milk, and egg free. See page 96)

For 6 servings use 10–12 small to medium parsnips. Pare and cut in half. Boil in salted water until tender. Drain.

Into a shallow baking dish large enough to lay parsnips without overlapping pour about ½ c. half-and-half or Cream Rich. Lay parsnips in cream. Sprinkle lightly with salt, paprika, and ⅛ tsp. dry mustard. Pour ¼ c. honey over parsnips. Top with ⅓ c. buttered bread crumbs (plain crumbs for milkless and wheatless bread for wheat free). Bake at 350° 15–20 min.

PARSNIPS WITH HERBS
(wheat, milk, and egg free)

Prepare and boil parsnips as above. In a heavy frying pan melt 4 T. margarine, or for milkless use vegetable shortening, olive oil, or bacon fat. Add ⅛ tsp. thyme. Brown the drained cooked parsnips in the fat. Sprinkle with a little salt, sugar, and minced parsley.

ZUCCHINI
(wheat, milk, and egg free)

Either slice or cut in half desired number of unpeeled zucchini. Allow 2 small or 1 medium to large half per serving. Cook, covered, in a small amount of water until just tender. These are very easy to overcook. Drain off any excess liquid. Sprinkle with onion and garlic powder and dot with butter or margarine. Use salad or olive oil or French salad dressing for milkless. Serve immediately.

STUFFED ZUCCHINI OR CROOK-NECKED SQUASH BOATS
(wheat, milk, and egg free)

Cook medium-size unpeeled squash whole in boiling salted water until just barely tender, about 10 min. Cut in half lengthwise and scoop out center, discarding seeds, and chop fine the remaining. The shell should be at least ¼ inch thick.

While the squash is cooking, brown ¼ lb. bulk sausage ¼ c. sliced mushrooms and 3 T. finely chopped onion. Drain off any excess fat. Add chopped squash, ½ c. fine bread crumbs or substitute (see Chap. 3) ⅓ c. grated Parmesan cheese (omit for milkless), ¼ tsp. thyme, ¼ tsp. salt, a dash of garlic powder, and pepper to taste. Mix well.

Spoon into squash shells. Sprinkle with 2 T. more Parmesan if allowed and with paprika. Bake at 350° 25–30 min.

ACORN SQUASH WITH HONEY BUTTER
(wheat, milk, and egg free)

Wash squash. Bake whole at 350–400° about 40 min. or until squash gives to the touch. Remove from oven. Cut in half, remove seeds and strings. Salt cavity and in each one put a spoon of honey and a spoon of butter or margarine. Use vegetable shortening and butter flavoring for milkless. Return to oven. Continue baking 10–15 min. or until squash is completely cooked. Most of the honey butter will be absorbed.

SWEET SOUR GLAZED CARROTS
(wheat, milk, and egg free)

In a small amount of salted water cook scraped young tender carrots whole, larger or older carrots sliced or cut in strips. Ideally, all the water is used in cooking. If not, drain, shake carrots gently in pan to help absorb last bit of water. Add a spoon of honey, butter (salad oil for milkless), and lemon juice. Heat should be very low. Shake carrots gently in pan to cover with juice. Cover a few minutes. They should be glazed. Grate a sprinkling of nutmeg over top and serve.

To give that little tantalizing something extra use Cointreau or Triple Sec instead of lemon and honey.

ARTICHOKE HEARTS WITH ROQUEFORT
(eggless and wheatless)

Use canned artichokes allowing 3–4 per serving. Drain off liquid; put into double boiler. Mash 2 T. butter and ¼ c. Roquefort or blue cheese together (for 1 can). Put over artichokes. Heat until cheese and butter are melted over artichokes and be sure they are hot.

So good and so different.

STUFFED MUSHROOMS
(wheat, milk, and egg free)

Lovely as an accompaniment to broiled chops. Allow 2–3 per serving.
Choose large brown mushrooms. Wash and pat dry quickly. Remove stems. Chop them fine. For 12 mushrooms: Brown ½ lb. lean ground sausage, ¼ c. chopped onion and the chopped stems. Drain off excess fat and pat with a paper towel to further remove fat. Stir in ⅓ c. wheat or cornbread crumbs (for wheatless bread see Chap. 3), and 2 T. chopped water chestnuts. Season to taste with salt, pepper, thyme, and marjoram. Mix well. Stuff cavities of mushrooms. Place in baking dish. Pour enough chicken broth or broth and sherry in dish to cover bottom. Add more during baking if necessary but don't soak mushrooms. Bake 30 min. at 350°.

SWEDISH BAKED POTATOES
(egg and wheat free)

Choose medium-size potatoes, allowing one per serving. Boil 10–15 min. Remove from stove. They will still be hard. Peel. Cradle potato in a large spoon and cut ¼ inch slices through potato to the spoon. (The spoon prevents cutting clear through and holds potato together.) Place potatoes in a buttered baking dish. Put butter or margarine into cuts. Sprinkle with salt. Bake at 425° 30–40 min. Remove from oven. Put buttered crumbs (See Chap. 3 for wheatless breads) and Parmesan cheese into cuts. Return to oven. Continue baking 15–20 min. or until done. Sprinkle with more Parmesan (optional).

YAMS IN WINE SAUCE
(wheat, milk, and egg free)

A delightful change from candied yams.
For 6–8 servings boil or bake 6 medium-size yams. Peel and cut crosswise into ⅜-inch slices. Arrange overlapped in shallow casserole.

In a small saucepan combine ⅓ c. sugar, ½ c. loganberry or blackberry wine* and 5 T. butter, margarine or vegetable shortening and butter flavoring. Boil rapidly, stirring, until bubbles are large and shining. Pour mixture evenly over yams. Bake at 375° for 20 min. or until yams are hot and sauce is bubbling. Serve sauce with yams.

SUGGESTED VARIATIONS FOR VEGETABLES

Peas: Add a little sugar, grated orange rind and mint.
Add chopped mushrooms and water chestnuts.
Add chopped celery or celery root simmered in chicken broth.
Limas: Add dill weed and butter or dill and olive oil and lemon juice.
Green beans: Add crisp bacon or salt pork bits, mushrooms, and water chestnuts sliced.
Add sautéed onion rings or chopped green onions.
Add celery or celery root as for peas.
Acorn squash: Sausage stuffing. See Stuffed Mushrooms or Zucchini. Pineapple filling: Cook squash as for honey butter squash. After removing seeds scoop out most of edible squash. Mash. For 3 squash combine ⅓ c. butter or margarine (omit for milkless), ½ c. crushed pineapple, 2 T. dry sherry or orange juice, 2 T. brown sugar, ¼ tsp. grated nutmeg and 1 tsp. salt. Mix well. Return to squash shells and bake at 425° 15–20 min. Serves 6.

BAKED BEANS (wheat, milk and egg free)

This recipe is not traditional. It has no molasses! But so good. Soak 1 pt. dry navy beans overnight (for high altitude; not necessary for sea level). Boil beans on top of stove until skins curl

---

* Orange juice can be substituted for the wine.

when you blow on a bean, but not until soft. Drain. Put beans into bean pot or deep pan. Cover with following sauce.

Combine: ½ c. brown sugar, ¼ c. vinegar, 1 T. salt, 1 T. dry mustard, 1 tsp. pepper, ½ tsp. red pepper or paprika (optional), 1 c. tomato juice, catsup or soup. (Soup is preferable if permitted.) Poke a chunk of salt pork, bacon, or fresh pork such as a pork shank into top of beans and pour well mixed sauce over all.

Bake a long time—6–8 hrs. at 250° or until beans are done. Stir occasionally as they cook. Add more tomato juice or water if needed as they cook.

PIQUANT TOMATOES
(wheat, milk, and egg free)

In a saucepan mix together ¾ c. vinegar, 1¼ tsp. celery seeds, 1½ tsp. mustard seeds, ½ tsp. salt, 1 T. plus 1¼ tsp. sugar, ¼ c. water, and pepper to taste. Bring to a boil and boil hard for 1 min. While it is still good and hot, pour over 6 large ripe but firm peeled and quartered tomatoes, 1 red onion sliced in rings, and 1 sliced green pepper. Cool and let stand several hrs. in refrigerator. Before serving add a sliced peeled cucumber (optional).

Wonderful to replace a salad or as a relish.

HOT POTATO SALAD
(wheat, milk, and egg free)

A GREEK VERSION

Boil 2 lbs. potatoes. Peel and dice. Combine in a bowl and pour over hot potatoes: ½ c. olive oil, ¼ c. vinegar, 2 T. thinly sliced onion, ¼ tsp. salt, pepper to taste. Toss lightly and serve warm.

HOT POTATO SALAD WITH BACON

Prepare potatoes as above. Put into bowl. Add ⅓ c. finely chopped onion and ½ lb. diced crisp bacon.

In a saucepan combine and heat to simmering ¾ c. white wine vinegar, ⅓ c. bacon drippings, 1½ tsp. salt, dash of sugar. Pour over potatoes. Mix well without breaking potatoes. Keep warm, stirring occasionally, in a double boiler 20–30 min. while flavors blend.

NO-FAT JAPANESE SAUCES USED AS SALAD DRESSINGS
(wheat, milk, and egg free)

Sauce No. 1: A sweet vinegar sauce
Mix together ⅔ c. Japanese vinegar, ⅓ tsp. salt ¼ c. sugar and ¼ tsp. accent (optional).

Sauce No. 2: Combine: ½ c. Japanese vinegar, 2 T. water, 1–2 tsp. soy sauce, ¼ tsp. salt and ¼ tsp. accent.

Sauce No. 3: ½ c. Japanese vinegar, 3 T. water, 3 T. sugar, ¼ tsp. salt, 1 T. soy sauce and ¼ tsp. accent.

(No. 2 and No. 3 are more pungent and less sweet.)

They are all good for vegetable salad mixes; No. 3 is also good for sea food.

Suggested salad mix: chopped or diced green or red onion, celery, green pepper, dacon or plain radishes, tomatoes without the seeds.

Bean sprout salad: Pour boiling water over 2 c. fresh sprouts. Let stand 3 min. Drain into colander, rinse well with cold water. Add chopped celery, onion and cucumber. Add Japanese sauce No. 2. Refrigerate several hours.

SALAD DRESSINGS

Cottage cheese or yogurt-base cream dressings are excellent made with low-fat cheese and yogurt. A blender is especially helpful with the cheese.

COTTAGE CHEESE DRESSING
(eggless and gluten free)

Without a blender sieve cheese, add remaining ingredients. Whip until smooth

2 c. cottage cheese, 1 c. buttermilk, no-fat or plain milk. Buttermilk is best.
3 T. mild vinegar, and 1 T. dry white wine or 4 T. wine vinegar, 4 tsp. packaged salad mix (blue cheese, Caesar, Italian, etc.).
Yield: 1½ pt. Store in refrigerator. This thickens slightly as it stands. Thin, if desired, with a little more milk.

THOUSAND ISLAND DRESSING
(eggless and gluten free)

Combine, in blender, or sieve cheese first, and whirl or stir until well mixed
　　　2 c. cottage cheese, ½ c. buttermilk or skim milk, 4 T. catsup, 4 T. mild vinegar.
Remove from blender. Add 6 T. chopped pickles or pickle relish, 1½ tsp. finely chopped green onion using part of the green.

ORANGE SALAD DRESSING
(eggless and gluten free)

Primarily for fruit salads. Combine in blender. Whirl until well mixed
　　　2 T. orange marmalade, 1 c. cottage cheese, ¼ c. buttermilk or milk, 3 T. lemon juice
Yogurt can be substituted for the cottage cheese and milk. Reduce lemon juice to taste.

YOGURT FRUIT SALAD DRESSING
(eggless and gluten free)

Mix together
　　　1 c. plain low fat yogurt, 2 T. mild honey,
　　　4 tsp. fresh mint (finely chopped), or
　　　3 tsp. dried mint leaves, 2 tsp. lemon juice

YOGURT ROQUEFORT DRESSING
(eggless and gluten free)

Combine, in blender or by hand, 1 c. low-fat yogurt, 3–4 T. Roquefort or blue cheese (room temperature), about ½ tsp. salt, ¼ tsp. Worcestershire.
For hand mixing, mash cheese with fork, then add yogurt. Beat until smooth.

BOILED DRESSING
(eggless and gluten free)

Measure and mix in pan 2 T. sugar, 1 tsp. dry mustard, ½ tsp. salt, 2 T. cornstarch, dash of paprika.
Gradually add ½ c. water
Cook, stirring, over medium heat until mixture is thick and cornstarch is thoroughly cooked.
Remove from heat. Gradually add 1 T. vinegar, ¼ c. (½ stick) margarine.
Blend in well. Gradually add ⅔ c. buttermilk. Stir until mixture is smooth and creamy. Store in refrigerator. For a thicker dressing increase cornstarch to 2½ T.
Variations:
Thousand Island. Add chili sauce or catsup, pickle relish, chopped green pepper (optional), chopped stuffed olives (optional) to the thicker dressing.
Caper Dressing: Add 1–2 T. chopped capers, ½ tsp. mustard seed to 1 c. dressing. Let stand to soften mustard seeds.
Dill Dressing: Add dill weed to taste. Try 2 tsp. to 1 c. dressing.
Horseradish Sauce or dressing: Add eggless horseradish sauce to taste. Try 2–3 T. Good with meat or vegetable salads, or ham or corned beef.
Poppy Seed Dressing: Add about 1 T. poppy seeds, 2 T. honey, and a little onion powder, 1 T. catsup (optional).
Curry Dressing: Add curry powder to taste.

"EGGLESS MAYONNAISE"
(eggless and gluten free)

A most satisfactory dressing. All ingredients should be thoroughly chilled before mixing. Work as rapidly as possible. If mixer is used, chill bowl and beaters before starting; if mixing by hand, set cold bowl in pan of ice water.

Mix together   1 tsp. sugar, 1 tsp. salt, ⅓ tsp. paprika, 1 tsp. dry mustard.

Add   ¼ c. undiluted evaporated milk, then ⅓ c. salad oil a tsp. at a time.

Beat well after each addition.

Mix together   3 tsp. vinegar, 3 tsp. lemon juice

Add in small amounts alternately with ⅔ c. salad oil beating well after each addition. Store, covered, in refrigerator.

Yield: 1½ c.

COOKED FRUIT SALAD DRESSING
(eggless, milkless, and gluten free)

Mix in pan   1 c. sugar, 1 T. flour or 2 tsp. cornstarch, 1 tsp. salt.

Blend in the juice of 2 oranges, 1 lemon, and enough pineapple juice to make 1⅓ c.

Cook over medium heat, stirring, until slightly thickened and flour or cornstarch is cooked. Store in refrigerator, covered.

Yield: About 1½ c.

HONEY FRUIT FRENCH DRESSING
(eggless, milkless, and gluten free)

In a bowl or jar put ½ c. salad oil, ¾ tsp. salt, ½ tsp. paprika, 1 T. honey.

Mix together   2 T. orange juice, 2 T. grapefruit juice, 1 T. lemon juice, ½ tsp. vinegar.

Shake well before using. Store in refrigerator.

MOCK SOUR CREAM

Put in blender 3 T. lemon juice, 3 T. liquid skim milk or
fat free buttermilk.
Add gradually while on low speed 8 oz. low-fat or regular
cottage cheese. Blend several min. on high speed. If cream becomes too thick on standing, thin with milk to desired consistency.

SOUPS

NEW ENGLAND CLAM CHOWDER
(wheat, egg, and milk free)*

A delicious meal in itself.

To 1 qt. milk or cream rich add 4 crumbled soda crackers.
(For wheatless, thicken milk slightly with 2–3 T. potato or rice
flour.) Fry out ¼ lb. finely chopped salt pork or ½ lb. bacon.
Remove to a paper towel and pat out excess grease. Pour off all
but 2 T. drippings. In the drippings, cook until soft and golden
1 medium-size onion. Drain 3 (7½ oz.) cans minced clams. Set
aside the clams. To clam liquid add enough water or bottled
clam juice to make 3 c. Put into a 2-qt. saucepan. Bring to boil.
Add 2½ c. diced raw potato and the onion. (Onion powder may
be substituted for the onion, in which case save no drippings and
eliminate that step.) Simmer until potato is tender. Add clams
and milk or cream rich. Turn down heat. The mixture should
heat without boiling, slowly, to blend flavors. Add salt and pepper
to taste. Add 2 T. butter or margarine (omit for milkless).

MANHATTAN CHOWDER
(wheat, milk, and egg free)

Substitute 3 c. cooked tomatoes or tomato juice for milk.
Proceed as above.

---
* See page 96.

OYSTER STEW
(wheat, egg, and milk free)*

Fresh or canned oysters may be used. For 2 large servings use 1 8-oz. can small oysters or 1 10-oz. bottle fresh. For fresh oysters, reserve any liquid and add to milk. Heat oysters in skillet until edges curl. If medium or large size, cut into smaller pieces.

Add 1 pt. warm milk or cream rich. The milk may be thickened slightly with crushed soda crackers or potato or rice flour if desired. Add a little onion powder, a dash of A-1, salt and pepper to taste. Add a dab of butter just before serving where allowed. Heat gently but do not boil.

For canned oysters prepare milk as above and empty contents of can into milk. Heat gently as above.

CREOLE GUMBO
(wheat, milk, and egg free)

A delicious meal. For 12 servings:

Slowly fry 2½ c. canned okra in 3 T. drippings or shortening. Add 1 large chopped onion, 2 cloves chopped garlic, and 1 chopped green pepper. Fry until onion is soft. Add 2 T. wheat or potato flour. Blend. Add 1 8-oz. can tomato hot sauce. Mix well.

Add 1 c. cleaned shrimp, 1 c. crab meat, 1 pt. oysters and liquid (fish may be canned), 2 qts. hot water—slightly less if canned oysters used, 3 slices chopped bacon or 3 T. diced ham, 2 bay leaves, 2 sprigs parsley, 1 tsp. salt, pepper to taste, 1 tsp. thyme. Cook slowly for 1 hr. Gumbo should be thick and dark. Serve in soup bowls with a spoonful of hot cooked rice in center of each bowl.

CREAM OF SCALLOP SOUP
(wheat, egg, and milk free)*

Mix in a saucepan ½ tsp. dry mustard, ½ tsp. Worcestershire, ⅛ tsp. each garlic, onion, and celery powder.

---

* See page 96.

Add 2 8-oz. bottles clam nectar and 1 T. butter (omit for milkless).

Bring to a boil. Add ¾ lb. scallops cut into small pieces.

Simmer gently for 3 min.

Beat 2 egg yolks** with 1 c. half-and-half or Cream Rich.* Add a little of the hot mixture, stirring, then slowly add egg mixture to the scallop mixture stirring. Do not boil. Heat until hot and slightly thickened. Serve immediately with a dash of paprika and parsley. 4 servings.

JAMAICAN SQUASH SOUP
(wheat, milk, and egg free)

This is a national dish of Jamaica and when properly made is delicious. Good and bad are served even in Jamaica. The secret of the flavor seems to be in the variety of the squash. Our butternut may not be the same but gives the same results. The season on this squash is quite short compared to many varieties but it can be prepared and frozen for later use.

Peel squash, being sure to remove all strings. Steam in as little salted water as possible until tender. Mash with a fork and then put through food mill or into blender. Should be satiny smooth. This is important.

To make soup, combine 1 c. pureed squash, 1 12-oz. can clear chicken broth, ⅛ tsp. thyme, and ¼ tsp. onion powder. Blend well. Heat. Adjust salt if needed. Serve hot.

SOUP STOCK
(wheat, milk, and egg free)

Where commercial beef broth and consommé as well as most other canned soups are unusable for wheatless diets, and many

---

** For eggless soup reserve ¼ c. clam nectar. Make a paste with 2 t. flour or potato flour or cornstarch. Stir into mixture before half-and-half. Cook until slightly thickened. Add half-and-half and heat through. Serve as above.

* See page 96.

are for milkless the old-fashioned soup pot becomes most desirable. If small bones—both meat and fowl, meat trimmings, vegetable parings and trimmed leaves, celery tops, even pea pods are used, the stock becomes more economical, as even soup bones are amazingly dear these days. For soup, bones with a fair amount of meat are most desirable. For cooking stock, less is necessary.

Preparation: For 1½–2 qts. of stock use approximately 3 lbs. of bones—brisket, neck, oxtails, and/or trimmings. Sprinkle with salt and let stand about 1 hr. to bring out juices. To darken color of stock, cut off part of meat, sauté in hot fat until very brown and then add to pot after stock is boiling.

Cover bones and meat with 3 qts. of cold water. Let stand 30 min., then bring to boil. Skim to give a clearer broth.

Add 1 sliced onion, a couple of carrots cut in quarters, a handful of celery tops, 6–8 peppercorns, 2 large bay leaves, ¼ tsp. thyme, a little mace and allspice (optional), 1 c. tomatoes—fresh or canned, and whatever peelings or leaves you have. Let simmer 3–4 hrs. covered. The liquid should be reduced to about half. Taste and adjust seasoning. Strain, chill, remove fat. Remove meat pieces to return to soup. Discard the remains of the vegetables—they have done their job. The broth is ready to use. It will keep a week or 10 days in the refrigerator, indefinitely in the freezer.

VEGETABLE SOUP

Return meat pieces to stock. Add whatever vegetables are desired and simmer them until done in the stock.

LIMA BEAN OR SPLIT PEA SOUP
(wheat, milk, and egg free)

The stock* left from corned beef (see p. 143) or a ham bone covered with water and boiled with 1 sliced onion, 1 or 2 carrots, and a bay leaf are excellent for these soups.

---

* Check stock for saltiness. Dilute if very salty.

Lima Bean: Soak 1 c. dried limas over night in 3 c. water. Add to ham bone or corned beef stock and simmer, covered, about 1 hr. or until beans are very tender. Put through a food mill or colander to remove skins. Chill to skim off excess fat. Reheat and adjust flavors; add additional stock if desired, or tomato juice or strained tomatoes may be added.

Split Pea Soup: Follow directions for Lima Bean Soup.

CHICKEN OR TURKEY STOCK
(wheat, milk, and egg free)

The carcass plus any bits of meat make this soup stock. For a chicken add 4 c. water—for a turkey add 6 c. Cover and simmer 1 hr. Add ½ tsp. salt, celery leaves, parsley, lettuce leaves (optional), sliced onion and a carrot. Simmer another hr. Strain, chill, remove fat and use as stock.

For a richer stock or soup simmer a 4–5 lb. hen in 12 c. water for 2 hrs. Add vegetables as above and 1 tsp. salt. Continue simmering until chicken is very tender. Let chicken cool in broth, then remove. Strain the broth, remove grease. Use part of the chicken for chicken rice or noodle soup, or for Cream of Chicken Soup.

CREAM OF CHICKEN SOUP
(wheat, egg and milk free)*

Make a medium white sauce using half-and-half or Cream Rich. Thicken with flour or potato or rice flour. Add chicken pieces and chicken stock (see above) to desired thickness.

CHICKEN AVOCADO SOUP

Chop avocado into ¼ inch cubes and stir into cream of chicken soup. (See above). Allow 1 large avocado to 2 c. soup.

---

* See page 96.

BASIC CREAM SOUP
(wheat, egg, and milk free)*

Sauté 1 T. minced onion in 2 T. butter or bacon drippings until onion is soft—not brown.

Blend in 1½ T. flour or 1 T. potato or rice flour, ¼ tsp. salt and ⅛ tsp. paprika.

Stir in slowly and heat to the boiling point 1 c. rich milk or Cream Rich and 1 c. stock or vegetable water.

Add ¾–1 c. of the desired cooked vegetable minced, mashed, or finely chopped. Season to taste.

This may be made thicker or thinner by adjusting the amount of fluid.

TOMATO SOUP

Tomato soup presents a special problem. If not properly done it will curdle. The temperature of the milk and tomato must be the same, very hot, when they are combined. The tomato must be added slowly, stirring constantly, *to* the milk. Do not boil after combining. A double assurance against curdling is a *little* baking soda. Add it to the tomatoes. Allow to finish fizzing or bubbling before adding to the milk.

Proportions: 1 pt. strained tomatoes (stewed canned are excellent), tomato sauce or juice seasoned with onion, A-1, salt, pepper, basil, or to taste.

Add ¼ tsp. soda. Add to 1 qt. of medium white sauce or basic cream soup as above.

CHILLED AVOCADO SOUP
(egg and gluten free)

Combine in blender 1 c. *each* mashed ripe avocado, plain low fat yogurt, and undiluted beef or chicken consomme, canned or

---
* See page 96.

home made. Add 1 T. lemon juice, ¼ tsp. onion salt, ½ tsp. sugar, dash of salt, or to taste. Blend well. Pepper optional. Add a drop of green coloring if desired but be careful. Chill thoroughly. Finely chopped crisp bacon and chopped chives may be added to individual servings as garnish. A hand rotary beater may replace blender. Serves 4–6.

Index

181